*Clifford R. O'Donnell*
*Joseph R. Ferrari*
*Editors*

D1149907

# Employment in Community Psychology: The Diversity of Opportunity

*Employment in Community Psychology: The Diversity of Opportunity* has been co-published simultaneously as *Journal of Prevention & Intervention in the Community*, Volume 19, Number 2 2000.

*Pre-publication*
*REVIEWS,*
*COMMENTARIES,*
*EVALUATIONS . . .*

"**F**ascinating and instructive reading, indeed a must read for all community psychology faculty, students, and potential employers. Sixteen community psychologists offer compelling, diverse, and unique perspectives on their employment journeys."

**Kenneth I. Maton, PhD**
*Professor of Psychology,*
*Director, Community-Social*
*PhD Program in Human*
*Services Psychology*
*President (1999-2000), Society*
*for Community Research*
*and Action*
*University of Maryland*

*More pre-publication*
*REVIEWS, COMMENTARIES, EVALUATIONS . . .*

"**T**his book fills a gap in the field. Both my undergraduate and graduate students ask me where one works and what one does in community psychology. This book provides some answers in a very understandable form. . . . I especially like the variety of settings and applications that are illustrated."

**J. R. Newbrough, PhD**
*Professor
Department of Psychology
and Human Development
Vanderbilt University*

The Haworth Press, Inc.

# Employment in Community Psychology: The Diversity of Opportunity

*Employment in Community Psychology: The Diversity of Opportunity* has been co-published simultaneously as *Journal of Prevention & Intervention in the Community*, Volume 19, Number 2 2000.

# The *Journal of Prevention & Intervention in the Community*™ Monographic "Separates" (formerly the *Prevention in Human Services* series)*

For information on previous issues of *Prevention in Human Services*, edited by Robert E. Hess, please contact: The Haworth Press, Inc., 10 Alice Street, Binghamton, NY 13904-1580 USA.

Below is a list of "separates," which in serials librarianship means a special issue simultaneously published as a special journal issue or double-issue *and* as a "separate" hardbound monograph. (This is a format which we also call a "DocuSerial.")

"Separates" are published because specialized libraries or professionals may wish to purchase a specific thematic issue by itself in a format which can be separately cataloged and shelved, as opposed to purchasing the journal on an on-going basis. Faculty members may also more easily consider a "separate" for classroom adoption.

"Separates" are carefully classified separately with the major book jobbers so that the journal tie-in can be noted on new book order slips to avoid duplicate purchasing.

You may wish to visit Haworth's website at . . .

## http://www.haworthpressinc.com

. . . to search our online catalog for complete tables of contents of these separates and related publications.

You may also call 1-800-HAWORTH (outside US/Canada: 607-722-5857), or Fax 1-800-895-0582 (outside US/Canada: 607-771-0012), or e-mail at:

## getinfo@haworthpressinc.com

---

*Employment in Community Psychology: The Diversity of Opportunity*, edited by Joseph R. Ferrari, PhD, and Clifford R. O'Donnell, PhD (Vol. 19, No. 2, 2000). *"Fascinating and instructive reading, indeed a must read for all community psychology faculty, students, and potential employers. Sixteen community psychologists offer compelling, diverse, and unique perspectives on their employment journeys." (Kenneth I. Maton, PhD, Professor of Psychology, University of Maryland)*

*Contemporary Topics in HIV/AIDS Prevention*, edited by Doreen D. Salina, PhD (Vol. 19, No. 1, 2000). *Helps researchers and psychologists explore specific methods of improving HIV/AIDS prevention research.*

*Educating Students to Make-a-Difference: Community-Based Service Learning*, edited by Joseph R. Ferrari, PhD, and Judith G. Chapman, PhD (Vol. 18, No. 1/2, 1999). *"There is something here for everyone interested in the social psychology of service-learning." (Frank Bernt, PhD, Associate Professor, St. Joseph's University)*

*Program Implementation in Preventive Trials,* edited by Joseph A. Durlak, PhD, and Joseph R. Ferrari, PhD (Vol. 17, No. 2, 1998). *"Fills an important gap in preventive research. . . . Highlights an array of important questions related to implementation and demonstrates just how good community-based intervention programs can be when issues related to implementation are taken seriously." (Judy Primavera, PhD, Associate Professor of Psychology, Fairfield University, Fairfield, Connecticut )*

*Preventing Drunk Driving*, edited by Elsie R. Shore, PhD, and Joseph R. Ferrari, PhD (Vol. 17, No. 1, 1998). *"A must read for anyone interested in reducing the needless injuries and death caused by the drunk driver." (Terrance D. Schiavone, President, National Commission Against Drunk Driving, Washington, DC)*

*Manhood Development in Urban African-American Communities,* edited by Roderick J. Watts, PhD, and Robert J. Jagers (Vol. 16, No. 1/2, 1998). *"Watts and Jagers provide the much-needed foundational and baseline information and research that begins to philosophically and empirically validate the importance of understanding culture, oppression, and gender when working with males in urban African-American communities." (Paul Hill, Jr., MSW, LISW, ACSW, East End Neighborhood House, Cleveland, Ohio)*

***Diversity Within the Homeless Population: Implications for Intervention,*** edited by Elizabeth M. Smith, PhD, and Joseph R. Ferrari, PhD (Vol. 15, No. 2, 1997). *"Examines why homelessness is increasing, as well as treatment options, case management techniques, and community intervention programs that can be used to prevent homelessness." (American Public Welfare Association)*

***Education in Community Psychology: Models for Graduate and Undergraduate Programs,*** edited by Clifford R. O'Donnell, PhD, and Joseph R. Ferrari, PhD (Vol. 15, No. 1, 1997). *"An invaluable resource for students seeking graduate training in community psychology . . . [and will] also serve faculty who want to improve undergraduate teaching and graduate programs." (Marybeth Shinn, PhD, Professor of Psychology and Coordinator, Community Doctoral Program, New York University, New York, New York)*

***Adolescent Health Care: Program Designs and Services,*** edited by John S. Wodarski, PhD, Marvin D. Feit, PhD, and Joseph R. Ferrari, PhD (Vol. 14, No. 1/2, 1997). *Devoted to helping practitioners address the problems of our adolescents through the use of preventive interventions based on sound empirical data.*

***Preventing Illness Among People with Coronary Heart Disease,*** edited by John D. Piette, PhD, Robert M. Kaplan, PhD, and Joseph R. Ferrari, PhD (Vol. 13, No. 1/2, 1996). *"A useful contribution to the interaction of physical health, mental health, and the behavioral interventions for patients with CHD." (Public Health: The Journal of the Society of Public Health)*

***Sexual Assault and Abuse: Sociocultural Context of Prevention,*** edited by Carolyn F. Swift, PhD* (Vol. 12, No. 2, 1995). *"Delivers a cornucopia for all who are concerned with the primary prevention of these damaging and degrading acts." (George J. McCall, PhD, Professor of Sociology and Public Administration, University of Missouri)*

***International Approaches to Prevention in Mental Health and Human Services,*** edited by Robert E. Hess, PhD, and Wolfgang Stark* (Vol. 12, No. 1, 1995). *Increases knowledge of prevention strategies from around the world.*

***Self-Help and Mutual Aid Groups: International and Multicultural Perspectives,*** edited by Francine Lavoie, PhD, Thomasina Borkman, PhD, and Benjamin Gidron* (Vol. 11, No. 1/2, 1995). *"A helpful orientation and overview, as well as useful data and methodological suggestions." (International Journal of Group Psychotherapy)*

***Prevention and School Transitions,*** edited by Leonard A. Jason, PhD, Karen E. Danner, and Karen S. Kurasaki, MA* (Vol. 10, No. 2, 1994). *"A collection of studies by leading ecological and systems-oriented theorists in the area of school transitions, describing the stressors, personal resources available, and coping strategies among different groups of children and adolescents undergoing school transitions." (Reference & Research Book News)*

***Religion and Prevention in Mental Health: Research, Vision, and Action,*** edited by Kenneth I. Pargament, PhD, Kenneth I. Maton, PhD, and Robert E. Hess, PhD* (Vol. 9, No. 2 & Vol. 10, No. 1, 1992). *"The authors provide an admirable framework for considering the important, yet often overlooked, differences in theological perspectives." (Family Relations)*

***Families as Nurturing Systems: Support Across the Life Span,*** edited by Donald G. Unger, PhD, and Douglas R. Powell, PhD* (Vol. 9, No. 1, 1991). *"A useful book for anyone thinking about alternative ways of delivering a mental health service." (British Journal of Psychiatry)*

***Ethical Implications of Primary Prevention,*** edited by Gloria B. Levin, PhD, and Edison J. Trickett, PhD* (Vol. 8, No. 2, 1991). *"A thoughtful and thought-provoking summary of ethical issues related to intervention programs and community research." (Betty Tableman, MPA, Director, Division of Prevention Services and Demonstration Projects, Michigan Department of Mental Health, Lansing)*

***Career Stress in Changing Times,*** edited by James Campbell Quick, PhD, MBA, Robert E. Hess, PhD, Jared Hermalin, PhD, and Jonathan D. Quick, MD* (Vol. 8, No. 1, 1990). *"A well-organized book. . . . It deals with planning a career and career changes and the stresses involved." (American Association of Psychiatric Administrators)*

***Prevention in Community Mental Health Centers,*** edited by Robert E. Hess, PhD, and John Morgan, PhD* (Vol. 7, No. 2, 1990). *"A fascinating bird's-eye view of six significant programs of preventive care which have survived the rise and fall of preventive psychiatry in the U.S." (British Journal of Psychiatry)*

***Protecting the Children: Strategies for Optimizing Emotional and Behavioral Development,*** edited by Raymond P. Lorion, PhD* (Vol. 7, No. 1, 1990). *"This is a masterfully conceptualized and edited* *volume presenting theory-driven, empirically based, developmentally oriented prevention. " (Michael C. Roberts, PhD, Professor of Psychology, The University of Alabama)*

**The National Mental Health Association: Eighty Years of Involvement in the Field of Prevention,** edited by Robert E. Hess, PhD, and Jean DeLeon, PhD* (Vol. 6, No. 2, 1989). *"As a family life educator interested in both the history of the field, current efforts, and especially the evaluation of programs, I find this book quite interesting. I enjoyed reviewing it and believe that I will return to it many times. It is also a book I will recommend to students." (Family Relations)*

**A Guide to Conducting Prevention Research in the Community: First Steps,** by James G. Kelly, PhD, Nancy Dassoff, PhD, Ira Levin, PhD, Janice Schreckengost, MA, AB, Stephen P. Stelzner, PhD, and B. Eileen Altman, PhD* (Vol. 6, No. 1, 1989). *"An invaluable compendium for the prevention practitioner, as well as the researcher, laying out the essentials for developing effective prevention programs in the community. . . . . This is a book which should be in the prevention practitioner's library, to read, re-read, and ponder." (The Community Psychologist)*

**Prevention: Toward a Multidisciplinary Approach,** edited by Leonard A. Jason, PhD, Robert D. Felner, PhD, John N. Moritsugu, PhD, and Robert E. Hess, PhD* (Vol. 5, No. 2, 1987). *"Will not only be of intellectual value to the professional but also to students in courses aimed at presenting a refreshingly comprehensive picture of the conceptual and practical relationships between community and prevention." (Seymour B. Sarason, Associate Professor of Psychology, Yale University)*

**Prevention and Health: Directions for Policy and Practice,** edited by Alfred H. Katz, PhD, Jared A. Hermalin, PhD, and Robert E. Hess, PhD* (Vol. 5, No. 1, 1987). *Read about the most current efforts being undertaken to promote better health.*

**The Ecology of Prevention: Illustrating Mental Health Consultation,** edited by James G. Kelly, PhD, and Robert E. Hess, PhD* (Vol. 4, No. 3/4, 1987). *"Will provide the consultant with a very useful framework and the student with an appreciation for the time and commitment necessary to bring about lasting changes of a preventive nature." (The Community Psychologist)*

**Beyond the Individual: Environmental Approaches and Prevention,** edited by Abraham Wandersman, PhD, and Robert E. Hess, PhD* (Vol. 4, No. 1/2, 1985). *"This excellent book has immediate appeal for those involved with environmental psychology . . . likely to be of great interest to those working in the areas of community psychology, planning, and design." (Australian Journal of Psychology)*

**Prevention: The Michigan Experience,** edited by Betty Tableman, MPA, and Robert E. Hess, PhD* (Vol. 3, No. 4, 1985). *An in-depth look at one state's outstanding prevention programs.*

**Studies in Empowerment: Steps Toward Understanding and Action,** edited by Julian Rappaport, Carolyn Swift, and Robert E. Hess, PhD* (Vol. 3, No. 2/3, 1984). *"Provides diverse applications of the empowerment model to the promotion of mental health and the prevention of mental illness." (Prevention Forum Newsline)*

**Aging and Prevention: New Approaches for Preventing Health and Mental Health Problems in Older Adults,** edited by Sharon P. Simson, Laura Wilson, Jared Hermalin, PhD, and Robert E. Hess, PhD* (Vol. 3, No. 1, 1983). *"Highly recommended for professionals and laymen interested in modern viewpoints and techniques for avoiding many physical and mental health problems of the elderly. Written by highly qualified contributors with extensive experience in their respective fields." (The Clinical Gerontologist)*

**Strategies for Needs Assessment in Prevention,** edited by Alex Zautra, Kenneth Bachrach, and Robert E. Hess, PhD* (Vol. 2, No. 4, 1983). *"An excellent survey on applied techniques for doing needs assessments. . . It should be on the shelf of anyone involved in prevention." (Journal of Pediatric Psychology)*

**Innovations in Prevention,** edited by Robert E. Hess, PhD, and Jared Hermalin, PhD* (Vol. 2, No. 3, 1983). *An exciting book that provides invaluable insights on effective prevention programs.*

**Rx Television: Enhancing the Preventive Impact of TV,** edited by Joyce Sprafkin, Carolyn Swift, PhD, and Robert E. Hess, PhD* (Vol. 2, No. 1/2, 1983). *"The successful interventions reported in this volume make interesting reading on two grounds. First, they show quite clearly how powerful television can be in molding children. Second, they illustrate how this power can be used for good ends." (Contemporary Psychology)*

**Early Intervention Programs for Infants,** edited by Howard A. Moss, MD, Robert E. Hess, PhD, and Carolyn Swift, PhD* (Vol. 1, No. 4, 1982). *"A useful resource book for those child psychiatrists, paediatricians, and psychologists interested in early intervention and prevention." (The Royal College of Psychiatrists)*

***Helping People to Help Themselves: Self-Help and Prevention,*** edited by Leonard D. Borman, PhD, Leslie E. Borck, PhD, Robert E. Hess, PhD, and Frank L. Pasquale* (Vol. 1, No. 3, 1982). *"A timely volume . . . a mine of information for interested clinicians, and should stimulate those wishing to do systematic research in the self-help area." (The Journal of Nervous and Mental Disease)*

***Evaluation and Prevention in Human Services,*** edited by Jared Hermalin, PhD, and Jonathan A. Morell, PhD* (Vol. 1, No. 1/2, 1982). *Features methods and problems related to the evaluation of prevention programs.*

*Employment in Community Psychology: The Diversity of Opportunity* has also been published as *Journal of Prevention & Intervention in the Community*, Volume 19, Number 2 2000.

Cover design by Thomas J. Mayshock Jr.

The Haworth Press, Inc., 10 Alice Street, Binghamton, NY 13904-1580 USA

**Library of Congress Cataloging-in-Publication Data**

Employment in community psychology : the diversity of opportunity / Clifford R. O'Donnell, Joseph R. Ferrari, editors
       p. cm.
    Includes bibliographical references and index.
    ISBN 0-7890-0757-6 (alk. paper) – ISBN 0-7890-1036-4 (alk. paper)
    1. Community psychology–Vocational guidance I. O'Donnell, Clifford R. II. Ferrari, Joseph R.
RA790.55 .E47 2000
362.2–dc21                                         00-028115

# Employment
# in Community Psychology:
# The Diversity of Opportunity

Clifford R. O'Donnell
Joseph R. Ferrari
Editors

*Employment in Community Psychology: The Diversity of Opportunity* has been co-published simultaneously as *Journal of Prevention & Intervention in the Community*, Volume 19, Number 2 2000.

The Haworth Press, Inc.
New York • London • Oxford

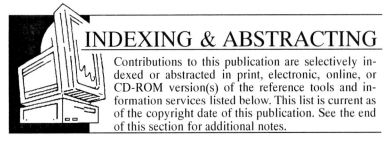

# INDEXING & ABSTRACTING

Contributions to this publication are selectively indexed or abstracted in print, electronic, online, or CD-ROM version(s) of the reference tools and information services listed below. This list is current as of the copyright date of this publication. See the end of this section for additional notes.

- *Abstracts of Research in Pastoral Care & Counseling*

- *Behavioral Medicine Abstracts*

- *BUBL Information Service, An Internet-based Information Service for the UK higher education community <URL: http://bubl.ac.uk/>*

- *Child Development Abstracts & Bibliography*

- *CNPIEC Reference Guide: Chinese National Directory of Foreign Periodicals*

- *EMBASE/Excerpta Medica*

- *Family Studies Database (online and CD/ROM)*

- *HealthPromis*

- *IBZ International Bibliography of Periodical Literature*

- *Mental Health Abstracts (online through DIALOG)*

- *National Center for Chronic Disease Prevention & Health Promotion (NCCDPHP)*

- *National Clearinghouse on Child Abuse & Neglect*

- *NIAAA Alcohol and Alcohol Problems Science Database (ETOH)*

- *OT BibSys*

- *Psychological Abstracts (PsycINFO)*

- *Referativnyi Zhurnal (Abstracts Journal of the All-Russian Institute of Scientific and Technical Information)*

- *RMDB DATABASE (Reliance Medical Information)*

(continued)

- *Social Planning/Policy & Development Abstracts (SOPODA)*

- *Social Work Abstracts*

- *Sociological Abstracts (SA)*

- *SOMED (social medicine) Database*

- *Violence and Abuse Abstracts: A Review of Current Literature on Interpersonal Violence (VAA)*

*Special Bibliographic Notes related to special journal issues (separates) and indexing/abstracting:*

- indexing/abstracting services in this list will also cover material in any "separate" that is co-published simultaneously with Haworth's special thematic journal issue or DocuSerial. Indexing/abstracting usually covers material at the article/chapter level.
- monographic co-editions are intended for either non-subscribers or libraries which intend to purchase a second copy for their circulating collections.
- monographic co-editions are reported to all jobbers/wholesalers/approval plans. The source journal is listed as the "series" to assist the prevention of duplicate purchasing in the same manner utilized for books-in-series.
- to facilitate user/access services all indexing/abstracting services are encouraged to utilize the co-indexing entry note indicated at the bottom of the first page of each article/chapter/contribution.
- this is intended to assist a library user of any reference tool (whether print, electronic, online, or CD-ROM) to locate the monographic version if the library has purchased this version but not a subscription to the source journal.
- individual articles/chapters in any Haworth publication are also available through the Haworth Document Delivery Service (HDDS).

# ABOUT THE EDITORS

**Clifford R. O'Donnell, PhD,** is Professor of Psychology at the University of Hawaii, where he serves as the Director of the Community and Culture Graduate Program. He is also a board member of the Melissa Institute for the Prevention and Treatment of Violence. Dr. O'Donnell has been Principal Investigator or Co-Principal Investigator on 17 projects and has written extensively on the subjects of delinquency prevention, firearm deaths among children and youths, social networks, programs for at-risk youths, community intervention, and culturally-compatible forms of community development. He has also served as a consultant to the United States Peace Corps, Head Start Hawaii, and has provided U.S. Congressional testimony and briefings about the United Nations Convention on the Rights of Children. In addition, Dr. O'Donnell was awarded fellow status in the Society for Community Research and Action (Division 27 of the American Psychological Association) in 1996 and received an award for his "Dedication and Support" from the Melissa Institute in 1998.

**Joseph R. Ferrari, PhD,** is Associate Professor in the Department of Psychology at DePaul University in Chicago, Illinois, and Editor-in-Chief of *Journal of Prevention & Intervention in the Community* since 1995. Dr. Ferrari received his PhD from Adelphi University in New York with a concentration in experimental social-personality psychology. His interest in this field includes persuasion, attribution theory, altruism, chronic procrastination, forgiveness, and shame/guilt processes. Dr. Ferrari has also developed several lines of research in applied social-community psychology in the areas of caregiver stress and satisfaction, the psychological sense of community, behavior analysis applied to community issues, recovery homes for addicts, welfare-to-work programs, and volunteerism and community service. In addition, he has published over 75 refereed articles, 8 scholarly books, and has made over 115 professional conference presentations.

# Employment in Community Psychology: The Diversity of Opportunity

## CONTENTS

# Employment Opportunities in Community Research and Action

Clifford R. O'Donnell

University of Hawaii

Joseph R. Ferrari

DePaul University

**KEYWORDS.** Employment, community psychology

Undergraduate students, upon first learning about community psychology, often ask "What can you do with a graduate degree in community psychology?" and "Who employs community psychologists?" Indeed, faculty colleagues usually ask the same questions when competing for the allocation of a new faculty position. The purpose of this book and special volume is to address these questions through examples of graduates educated in community psychology and employed in diverse applied, research, and academic settings. This special volume and book on employment is also a follow-up of our work on education in community psychology, which reviewed undergraduate courses and graduate programs in the field (O'Donnell & Ferrari, 1997a).

The usual answer to questions of employment in community psychology, that most positions are outside of academia, are not advertised in the *APA Monitor,* and do not have the title of community psychologist, typically brings puzzled, if not skeptical, looks. There-

---

Address corespondence to: Clifford R. O'Donnell, University of Hawaii, Honolulu, HI 96822.

[Haworth co-indexing entry note]: "Employment Opportunities in Community Research and Action." O'Donnell, Clifford R., and Joseph R. Ferrari. Co-published simultaneously in *Journal of Prevention & Intervention in the Community* (The Haworth Press, Inc.) Vol. 19, No. 2, 2000, pp. 1-4; and: *Employment in Community Psychology: The Diversity of Opportunity* (ed: Clifford R. O'Donnell, and Joseph R. Ferrari) The Haworth Press, Inc., 2000, pp. 1-4. Single or multiple copies of this article are available for a fee from The Haworth Document Delivery Service [1-800-342-9678, 9:00 a.m. - 5:00 p.m. (EST). E-mail address: getinfo@haworthpressinc.com].

fore, in this special volume/book, a "talk story" format is used. "Talk story" is a form of discourse common to Polynesian and Micronesian cultures in which meaning and culture is conveyed through the stories that people tell. In one form or another, it is used in all cultures in which oral history is important. It is hoped that the stories that these authors tell will convey an understanding of employment in community research and action that cannot be obtained through abstract description alone.

In telling their stories, the authors were asked to include information, as appropriate, on their graduate school experiences in community psychology and life that made them suitable for and are most helpful in their current positions, on how they conducted their searches for employment and obtained their positions, a description of their positions, duties, and activities, on what makes their positions interesting, and on the concepts of community psychology that are emphasized in their positions.

The authors range from current graduate students to psychologists well-established in positions in community research and action. The four graduate students, Robert Ahlen-Widoe, Natalie Contos, Susan M. Wolfe, and Carol Yakish, have all chosen interesting work in their fields, as an associate researcher in a university family research center, research consultant for Indigenous people, independent research and evaluation consultant, and an itinerant social worker for a regional Native non-profit health corporation respectively, that helps to employ them through graduate school, qualify them for future employment, and provide them with important experience that cannot be obtained in graduate school alone.

After graduate school, the next step, of course, is that important first position. Two of these articles address this process. In the first, Rebecca Campbell, Holly Angelique, Bonnie J. BootsMiller, and William S. Davidson II describe the creation and process of using a job club to obtain employment in both academic and applied positions. In the second, Kathryn Nemec, Ruth Hungerford, Linda Hutchings, and Ingrid Huygens provide overall information on the employment experiences on almost all of the community psychology graduates in New Zealand, with two case studies.

Most of the employment opportunities in community research and action are in applied positions. The four authors representing these positions illustrate the application of community psychology principles, the impact community psychologists can have on community social services, and the importance of research in applied settings: John Kalafat in several of his positions in applied settings, including school systems, a university campus, and a community hospital; David A. Julian in his position for planning, evaluation and research at a local United Way; Benjamin Kerman in a program evaluation and prevention position at a child welfare agency; and Deanna Parker Knapp as an operations manager of a university office of research, providing resources for researchers.

The research skills that students learn in community graduate programs are most important to qualify them for the diverse employment opportunities available to community psychologists. Often it is their research skills which are valued by the multi-disciplinary organizations who select graduates from many related fields. This is particularly true, of course, for multi-disciplinary research centers. These centers also provide opportunities for social impact on important issues through research, as exemplified by the work of Brian L. Wilcox on public policy as director of a university research center, Kurt M. Ribisl on tobacco control at a university school of medicine research center, Dale R. Fryxell on developmental disabilities at a University Affiliated Program (UAP), and HyunHee Chung in applying community psychology principles in Korean society at a private research institute, sponsored by a life insurance company, with the goal of promoting mental health through primary prevention.

The best known employment opportunities for community graduates, of course, are positions in academic departments at colleges and universities. In a development that has interesting implications for the field, an increasing number of these positions are outside of the departments of psychology (O'Donnell & Ferrari, 1997b). These positions are represented by David Henry in a tenure-track position in a department of psychiatry, with research in an institute of juvenile research, and Douglas D. Perkins in interdisciplinary programs in criminal justice and in environment, behavior, family, and consumer studies, with consultation to government and community organizations.

# REFERENCES

O'Donnell, C. R., & Ferrari, J. R. (Eds.) (1997a). *Education in community psychology: Models for graduate and undergraduate programs.* New York: The Haworth Press, Inc.

O'Donnell, C. R., & Ferrari, J. R. (1997b). Undergraduate courses and graduate programs in community research and action: Issues and future directions. In C. R. O'Donnell & J. R. Ferrari (Eds.), *Education in community psychology: Models for graduate and undergraduate programs* (pp. 97-99). New York: The Haworth Press, Inc.

# Twenty Cents and a New Way of Thinking

Robert Ahlen-Widoe

Institute for Families in Society
University of South Carolina

**SUMMARY.** The successful practice of community research and action may require thinking acquired through multi-disciplinary learning experiences. Community psychology has a tradition of exploring perspectives that promote effective relationships with community research and action, while still focusing on scientific traditions in research. Other learning experiences such as those provided in the arenas of urban and regional planning, education, qualitative research, and others doing community development can assist in expanding the "in the world" practice of community research and action. In exploring new ways of thinking and working with communities, it may be very important to begin to place more emphasis on having our practice inform our research. *[Article copies available for a fee from The Haworth Document Delivery Service: 1-800-342-9678. E-mail address: getinfo@haworthpressinc.com <Website: http://www.haworthpressinc.com>]*

**KEYWORDS.** Community psychology, multi-disciplinary, activity settings, asset

Even before graduate school, I talked–perhaps too frequently–about the importance of new paradigms for social services. At our "Aloha Party" just before we departed for the University of Hawaii in 1990, a

---

Address correspondence to: Robert Ahlen-Widoe, Institute for Families in Society, University of South Carolina, Columbia, SC 29208.

[Haworth co-indexing entry note]: "Twenty Cents and a New Way of Thinking." Ahlen-Widoe, Robert. Co-published simultaneously in *Journal of Prevention & Intervention in the Community* (The Haworth Press, Inc.) Vol. 19, No. 2, 2000, pp. 5-11; and: *Employment in Community Psychology: The Diversity of Opportunity* (ed: Clifford R. O'Donnell, and Joseph R. Ferrari) The Haworth Press, Inc., 2000, pp. 5-11. Single or multiple copies of this article are available for a fee from The Haworth Document Delivery Service [1-800-342-9678, 9:00 a.m. - 5:00 p.m. (EST). E-mail address: getinfo@haworthpressinc. com].

friend of mine gave me a going-away card with two bright and shiny, government-issue ten cent pieces taped to the bottom. In an all too legible scrawl were the words, "This is probably the closest you're going to get to 'new pair-a-dimes'." I'm not sure yet whether he was right. However, I'd like to share some of my thoughts and experiences based on the possibility of new ways of thinking that I think I've carried into my work after graduate school.

I joined the Institute for Families in Society at the University of South Carolina as a Research Associate in July, 1995. I'd like to say that a long, arduous, and disciplined search led to the position, but it was more like being in the right place at the right time since the Institute was growing rapidly. I found the position by staying in touch with a former professor who had left the University of Hawaii to help start the Institute in late 1994. Electronic communication (e-mail, fax, and phone) gave me the ability to explore opening positions, possibilities, apply, and even interview by conference call from Hawaii.

The Institute is a university-affiliated research and action organization that is funded primarily by "soft money" (grants and contracts). It is not a part of any particular department, school, or college. It is a multi-disciplinary operation with multiple ties in multiple places throughout the university, public and private sectors, and is layered from local to international in scope. In simple terms, the work we do is designed to assist communities and organizations in providing effective services and supports to, and linkages with families. For the most part, we do not provide direct services or interventions with families. We work with the people who work with the people.

The scope of my own work has been multi-faceted and has included work in program evaluation, community consultation, organizational and systems change, development of technical assistance and training packages, and the design of processes that support community-based development activities. Before the Institute, I had a previous professional life. I worked for 24 years in juvenile justice as a counselor, supervisor, and an administrator–all of which involved working on individual, family, program, organizational, and systems levels. In academics, I am best described as a late bloomer, having earned my first degree in 1988 at age 46 and started graduate studies two years later.

## *MULTIPLICITY*

Recently our youngest daughter sent me a *Los Angeles Times* article on multi-disciplinary education that expressed the view that cross-disciplinary knowledge and education is the wave of the future. While I can't attest to the accuracy of this prediction, I can say that the multidisciplinary nature of the University of Hawaii Community Studies program has been one of the most useful features of my graduate education. This program covered learning experiences in community psychology and core work in psychology on the graduate level. Just as importantly, these experiences included several allied fields including urban and regional planning, education, qualitative research, cross- and inter-cultural psychology.

## *TEN CENTS FROM COMMUNITY PSYCHOLOGY*

The core traditions of psychological research and current publication standards in community psychology research have proved valuable. Nearly all federal, and some state and foundation-funded research grants, are grounded in the traditions of hard science research. Grant research and writing requires a working knowledge of these traditions. Since we operate on "soft money," these skills are essential.

Several community psychology perspectives and contexts for community work have proved very pertinent to my work. Rappaport (1984) has suggested that psychological thought has engaged in convergent thinking and that effective community solutions would be of a divergent nature, coming from the bottom up, with collaboration and gaining control on the part of the powerless as desired ends. This implies a breakdown of typical expert roles between the professional and the community. Along with this, I've found that a slight modification of Cochran's (1987) assumptions in working with families has been very useful. By inserting the word "communities" in place of families, these assumptions now read that all communities have strengths; community members are a source of expert-level knowledge about their communities even though they may not currently have the tools to implement that expertise; valid and useful knowledge about communities can be found in social networks, in ethnic and cultural traditions, and across generations; and there are a variety of legitimate community forms.

Katz (1984) talked about the "scarcity" paradigm in human resources and proposed instead a model of synergy. This view suggests a shift toward the development of community possibilities as generative and creative, rather than being limited to what currently exists. Without this kind of view, our work in seemingly resource-limited communities might be at a complete standstill. This perspective has also assisted in providing a useful segue from a problem-based to an asset-based approach to community development. Communities appreciate and resonate well with these assumptions and perspectives, and many have started to become "unstuck" as a result.

Some have proposed that cultures and their subgroups may be viewed as having a story or drama to be told (Rappaport, 1995; Trickett, 1996). I've found that stories and dramas provide valuable sources of information, context, and outcomes, and are also highly important in the transfer of information to communities about growth and development possibilities.

I regularly use organizational change notions of identifying and building on shared values and vision, the value of having a common point of departure for efforts, the benefits of participatory involvement and shared ownership, and a systems thinking perspective that leads to organizational and community learning. Learning organization principles (Senge, 1990) and soft-systems transformation (Checkland & Scholes, 1990) have proved vital to developing effective consulting relationships with community building efforts.

Finally, a theory from community psychology that has proved to be valuable has been the activity setting model developed by O'Donnell and Tharp (1990). Activity settings may be analyzed in terms of their component parts which are "(1) physical resources, (2) funds, (3) time, (4) symbols, (5) people, and (6) positions, centered around the activity of the setting" (1990, p. 258). These settings are nested in other larger settings which interact with the setting. This model has provided a very useful template for assisting and gauging the development of settings. Moreover, community members interested in developing effective resources and relationships have realized expanded possibilities for both through the use of this setting perspective.

## TEN CENTS FROM OTHER AREAS

In addition to the designs and research that are used in community psychology, I have found my learning experiences in the other disciplines to be highly useful. Qualitative research is becoming increasingly important. Many communities and community-based programs are looking for ways to collect data that help contextualize the information they've traditionally recorded and to find expanded ways of recording processes and results. Many of the perspectives and methods of naturalistic inquiry (Lincoln & Guba, 1985) have helped guide work with communities and organizations. Many communities and community-based programs want to find ways to evaluate their efforts and outcomes. Utilization focused evaluation perspectives (Patton, 1986) have proved very beneficial. In addition to quantitative data, we are finding qualitative and utilization principles are assisting us in the elaboration and expansion of empowerment evaluation work.

Planning studies in community-based development and social impact assessment have provided a real-world grounding in both research and practice. Community-based development introduced me to meaningful case studies, practical applications, successes and failure of efforts, the traditions and growth of community-based work, and new directions and perspectives in community research and action. In this area, probably the most important "new twenty-cents worth" has been the advent and development of asset-based community development (Kretzman & McKnight, 1993). This new way of thinking has led to the development of such useful tools and methods as asset inventories (frameworks of assets in different settings) and asset mapping (identifying and locating assets in physical space). People in communities here have embraced these ideas and perspectives, and in many instances are undertaking community-driven efforts to inventory, map, and effectively leverage community assets.

Also from the planning arena, social impact assessment (SIA) has provided very useful frameworks for gathering community descriptors and useful indicators to see where communities are now and where their growth may take them. SIA is also very helpful in the evaluation arena in terms of assisting to identify outcomes-based indicators. And make no mistake, *everyone* is using (or trying to use) outcomes and results-based perspectives for social service evaluation.

## DOES THIS ADD UP TO A NEW TWENTY CENTS?

Trickett (1996) has talked of the "discrepancy between the ways in which we construct our work for publication and the ways in which we actually conduct it" (p. 212). The ideas I've held closely and actually transferred from my graduate school experience into my current world of practice and research suggest that a new way of thinking is important to the advancement of community work and probably people-science as well.

This returns me to the original dilemma posed by my friend. Are we seeing the emergence of a new paradigm–or should I just be happy with the twenty cents? At this point, the jury is still out on how prophetic my friend may have been. However, as I look at what has been most useful in work with communities and organizations, and the new thought emerging in community psychology and allied fields, I'd have to say that *something* is going on. That something, together with Trickett's discrepancy above, lead me to wonder if maybe we have it backwards at times. Maybe one of the steps we should take in discovering additional connections with communities, research and action really should be to *talk our walk*–and thus let our actions inform our research in truly reciprocal ways.

## SO YOU WANT TO PRACTICE COMMUNITY PSYCHOLOGY

For those who are interested in working in community development arenas similar to those described above, I would like to offer several suggestions. First, pay close attention to the traditions of research and action, while still looking for those ideas and practices which will provide you with the most effective connections with diverse communities. Second, get out of your own discipline and explore the learning possibilities of other fields doing similar work. The goal here is to collect a large toolkit to fit the contexts of your work with communities. There are three other things that are important: practice, practice, practice. This means putting yourself in as many positions as possible to have your practice inform your research and vice versa. I would suggest these include not only practicum experience, but also whatever work and life experience that will immerse you in the learning perspectives needed to work with communities. Finally, learn to dance. Dance with new ideas, new people, old and new ways of thinking, and maybe with a new twenty cents in your pocket.

## REFERENCES

Cochran, M. (1987). Empowering families: An alternative to the deficit model. In K. Hurrelmann (Ed.) *Social intervention: Potential and constraints* (pp. 105-120). New York: de Gruyter.

Checkland, P. & Scholes, J. (1990). *Soft systems methodology in action.* Chichester: John Wiley & Sons.

Katz, R. (1984). Empowerment and synergy: Expanding the community's healing resources. In Rappaport, J., Swift, C. F., & Hess, R. (Eds.) *Studies in empowerment: Steps toward understanding and action* (pp. 201-225). New York: The Haworth Press, Inc.

Kretzmann, J. & McKnight, J. (1993). *Building communities from the inside out: A path toward finding and mobilizing a community's assets.* Chicago: ACTA Publications.

Lincoln, Y. S. & Guba, E. G. (1985). *Naturalistic Inquiry.* Beverly Hills: Sage.

O'Donnell, C. & Tharp, R. (1990). Community intervention guided by theoretical development. In A. S. Bellack, M. Hersen, & A. E. Kazdin (Eds.) *International handbook of behavior modification and therapy,* 2nd edition (pp. 251-266). New York: Plenum Press.

Patton, M. (1986). *Utilization-focused evaluation,* 2nd edition. Newbury Park: Sage Publications.

Rappaport, J. (1984). Studies in empowerment: Introduction to the issue. In Rappaport, J., Swift, C. F., & Hess, R. (Eds.) *Studies in empowerment: Steps toward understanding and action* (pp. 1-7). New York: The Haworth Press, Inc.

Rappaport, J. (1995). Empowerment means narrative: Listening to stories and creating settings. *American Journal of Community Psychology, 23, (5),* 795-807.

Senge, P. (1990). *The fifth discipline.* New York: Doubleday.

Trickett, E. (1996). A future for community psychology: The contexts of diversity and the diversity of contexts. *American Journal of Community Psychology, 24 (2),* 209-234.

# The Pinjarra Massacre Site Project: From Doctoral Student to Community Consultant

Natalie Contos

Curtin University of Technology
Perth, Western Australia

**SUMMARY.** The work described in this article came about as a result of the author's doctoral studies. What began as a program of action research developed into concrete social action dealing with issues of social justice and reconciliation between Indigenous and non-Indigenous groups in a town in Australia's Southwest. The strong collaborative partnerships that developed during the research process led to employment on a project concerned with promoting the recognition of a massacre of local Indigenous people in the early days of European invasion. While a community psychologist was not necessarily the obvious person for the job, the article demonstrates how key principles of community psychology guided the project, and were in fact vital for its success. *[Article copies available for a fee from The Haworth Document Delivery Service: 1-800-342-9678. E-mail address: getinfo@haworthpressinc.com <Website: http://www.haworthpressinc.com>]*

Address correspondence to: Natalie Contos, School of Psychology, Curtin University of Technology, GPO Box U1987, Perth, Western Australia, 6001.

The author would like to acknowledge Pinjarra Nyungar Community Leader and personal friend, Theo Kearing, who died in February of 1998. It was through his incredible vision, determination, and dedication to social justice for his people, that the Pinjarra Massacre Site Project became a reality. The author would also like to thank Brian Bishop, Chris Sonn and Harry Pickett for their guidance and support throughout the doctoral process.

[Haworth co-indexing entry note]: "The Pinjarra Massacre Site Project: From Doctoral Student to Community Consultant." Contos, Natalie. Co-published simultaneously in *Journal of Prevention & Intervention in the Community* (The Haworth Press, Inc.) Vol. 19, No. 2, 2000, pp. 13-19; and: *Employment in Community Psychology: The Diversity of Opportunity* (ed: Clifford R. O'Donnell, and Joseph R. Ferrari) The Haworth Press, Inc., 2000, pp. 13-19. Single or multiple copies of this article are available for a fee from The Haworth Document Delivery Service [1-800-342-9678, 9:00 a.m. - 5:00 p.m. (EST). E-mail address: getinfo@haworthpressinc.com].

*13*

**KEYWORDS.** Indigenous Australians, action research, social change, social justice reconciliation

The author recently began work in the field of community research and action while concurrently completing the last year of a doctorate in community psychology. The doctorate is concerned with issues of social justice and reconciliation between Indigenous and non-Indigenous groups in a town in the Southwest of Western Australia. Through the course of the research, a close relationship developed between the author and the Indigenous community. Then in June, 1997, the local Indigenous Association, Murray Districts Aboriginal Association (MDAA), employed the author as research consultant on a project of vital importance to their community: 'The Pinjarra Massacre Site Research and Development Project.'

The project concerns an incident known in White history as the 'Battle of Pinjarra,' where, at dawn on October 28, 1834, the local Aboriginal group were ambushed and massacred by British troops. The incident occurred just seven years after the British colonial settlement of Western Australia. The area now known as Pinjarra was occupied by the Bindjareb (Pinjarra) Nyungar people. They were a fierce group whose successful guerrilla tactics were posing a serious threat to the intended 'settlement' of the Pinjarra frontier, 100 kilometres south of Perth. Settlers throughout the colony were becoming increasingly insecure.

The 'Battle of Pinjarra' represented an attempt by the head of the colony (Governor James Stirling) to put an end to Aboriginal resistance to British invasion. The massacre sent a clear message to all Indigenous communities living throughout the Southwest: Should they dare act to resist the invasion of their lands, they would be shot.

Over one hundred and sixty years later, Australia as a nation is just beginning to grapple with the reality of its early history, and indeed, the continued oppression of Indigenous Australians in changing guises through to the present day. It is in this climate that MDAA have initiated their project, for the 'Battle of Pinjarra' to be recognized as the massacre that it really was. For the local Nyungar community, and symbolically, for the broader Indigenous community, the event is a concrete and powerful example of the violence perpetrated against their people by the colonisers of this country. While colonial records sought to minimise and rationalise the massacre, the fact that it happened is indisputable. Therefore, challenging white accounts and meanings of the massacre and gaining widespread recognition of the Nyungar experience of the event has become a crucial issue for the local Nyungar community. In psychological terms, it is a fight to redefine the event from the perspective of the Indigenous people; to give *voice* to their experience (Reinharz, 1994).

The Pinjarra Massacre Site Research and Development Project consists of a research phase aimed at redefining the event to include Nyungar perspectives, and a development phase in which a Memorial Area to the event would be established. The author had been involved with the community for almost two years when MDAA received funding for the research phase. Work on the research phase was to include the following tasks: Researching all literature and Nyungar as well as Wadjella (the Nyungar term for the Caucasian majority) oral and written histories of the Massacre; co-ordinating a ground survey to attempt to locate the burial sites of those Bindjareb Nyungars who had died in the Massacre (this would include negotiating with landowners for permission to survey); negotiating with the local Shire Council and other stakeholder organisations to promote and ensure Indigenous control of an area set aside for the commemoration of the Massacre; and developing promotional material about the event for schools and tourist agencies.

The doctoral research had been guided by the principles of substantive theorising (Wicker, 1989). This approach facilitated the development of a relationship of mutual respect and trust that ultimately led to employment with the community. The author's initial intent was to work alongside the Indigenous and non-Indigenous communities, and, in the role of participant conceptualizer (e.g., Smith, 1983), to explore issues of importance to them. A guiding principle was that researching particular issues in their context would enable the research to directly inform those particular issues in their context (e.g., Dokecki, 1992; Newbrough, 1992; Wicker, 1989). The commitment to *action* research was vital, because Indigenous Australians have been repeatedly exploited by researchers who have come, observed, and left, without 'giving back' in any tangible way to the communities they researched.

Entering a new community with such an intention is not easy. In the present case, as a Wadjella with a very different background to the Nyungar community, the author was confronted with unfamiliar structures and systems of meaning that caused considerable uncertainty and ambiguity. The temptation to 'take control,' to impose one's own values and meanings on the situation at hand, was hard to resist. The opportunity to reflect on events and values through discussions within a support structure external to the community, such as a thesis committee, was therefore vital. The committee provided encouragement to 'stay with' the feelings of impotence and uncertainty, and to engage in ongoing reflections on experiences in the context. This, combined with the patience of the Nyungar community, allowed for the development of an appreciation of the context from an *emic* perspective, and the process resulted in close collaborative ties between researcher and the community.

In fact the appreciation of context that had developed in the 2 year period prior to employment was somewhat akin to that of the 'resident researcher' (Wicker & Sommer, 1993), though the author had not actually lived in the community. Employment with the Nyungar community came about as a direct result of the collaborative ties that had been established during this time, and the success of the project has continued to depend on them (this is demonstrated later). When first offered the position, possession of the requisite skills to complete the work was a secondary (though obviously an important) factor, in comparison to the importance of the *relationship* that had been established between the author and the community. Indeed, the influence of relationship in the change process is not to be underestimated.

As a Wadjella and therefore a member of the dominant group, part of the process of ongoing reflection has related to the type of role appropriate to undertake. In the case of the Massacre Site Project, MDAA were absolutely clear about what they wanted to achieve; the author's role was to assist in the mechanics of realizing their goal. Accordingly, the work has been conducted in close collaboration with key members of the Indigenous community. Strategies for action have been developed in a dynamic way through ongoing discussions. All negotiations with outside stakeholders have been undertaken in partnership with key members of MDAA, with the exception of situations in which it was agreed that it would be politically better for the author to 'go it alone.' This tactic was useful, for example, in initial interactions with landowners who were suspicious of Indigenous motives.

This partnership approach to negotiations has resulted, amongst other things, in the strengthening of relationships between leaders of the local Indigenous community and other key stakeholders in the project (e.g., Shire representatives).

Facilitating a reframing of the issues on the part of the non-Indigenous community–both key stakeholders, and the wider local community-has been a central aspect of the author's work. Smith (1983) has advocated this as a vital tool for community change, and similarly, Huygens (1995) has stressed the importance of supporting the agendas of oppressed groups by encouraging such change in the oppressive group. The Pinjarra Massacre Site Project represents the culmination of various attempts by the Indigenous community to challenge white understandings of the Massacre of Pinjarra (starting with the very crucial issue of its title). The non-Indigenous response to past initiatives regarding the Massacre Site had been to reject this challenge–to construe the situation in terms of the Indigenous community 'dredging up the past,' attempting to blame the Wadjellas for the 'sins of their fathers,' and generally, 'make trouble.' Past initiatives had therefore been undermined by the Shire Council, and the community at large. The challenge, then, was to conduct the research phase of the Project in such a way as to encourage the non-Indigenous community to reframe the Indigenous initiative in terms that would unite, rather than divide the communities.

To this end, there has been a strong 'reconciliation' focus to the project. That is, an emphasis on the potential for the project to bring the Indigenous and non-Indigenous communities together through the acknowledgement of past hurts, and the hope of a brighter future together. Another point of influence has been the promise of mutual economic benefit through tourism.

To promote the reconciliatory focus of the project, the wider community was encouraged to participate in the annual day of commemoration of the Massacre ('Back to Pinjarra Day') in October, 1997. The local schools and church groups became highly involved in the day's events. In the lead up to the commemorative day, a display about the Massacre was erected in the local library, and a written survey distributed to gauge peoples' knowledge and perspectives on the Massacre within the local community. The survey information sheet described the project, emphasised its reconciliatory nature and invited community input. A summary of survey responses was then circulated within the community, which contrasted the negative rhetoric on the issue with the many informed, positive perspectives that were expressed by locals themselves. As a result of these measures, a shift in the framing of the Massacre Site Project by many local Wadjellas is becoming evident. Resistance to the project is decreasing, and support is increasing. The local Shire, for example, is now on our side.

Negotiations with landowners, the local Shire and other key stakeholders continue to be conducted in the spirit of reconciliation, with an emphasis on the mutual benefits of the project to the Indigenous and non-Indigenous communities. Future plans for the second phase of the project, the development of the Memorial Area, are being designed to involve the local community, both Indigenous and non-Indigenous.

In the course of work described above, people have frequently assumed that the author's background was in history, anthropology or archaeology rather than psychology. Indeed, a lack of experience with heritage issues was of concern at the outset. However, as the work nears completion, it has become clear that a background in community psychology was highly appropriate for the task at hand. The dual emphasis of the discipline on research and action: the guiding values of social justice and empowerment; the emphasis on facilitating negotiation between key stakeholders, and of community involvement, all have been vital. But perhaps most important and a guiding cornerstone of Australian community psychology, is the commitment to working within the frameworks of the local community themselves, weaving the practitioner's skills with local visions and cultural understandings to conduct all work in a truly collaborative manner (Bishop & Syme, 1992).

In Australia, there are few jobs advertised specifically for the 'community psychologist,' external to the university setting. To someone considering a career in community psychology, this can be rather daunting. However, the experience described above provides an example of the kind of work for which postgraduate training in community psychology prepares the individual, and to which such training can lead.

From a personal perspective, Pinjarra Nyungar community leaders and the author have discussed the possibility of continuing a working partnership beyond the present project, and are considering grants that may make this possible. The depth of understanding that has developed in this particular context would certainly enhance the quality of further work within the community. Beyond this context, there are various organisations concerned with the pursuit of justice and equity for Australia's Indigenous people; for example, in the areas of native title and reconciliation. Positions may involve working with non-Indigenous, dominant communities and structures, and/or Indigenous communities and structures in order to create positive social change. In such positions, a firm grounding in community psychology will have provided the framework and the tools necessary to be able to make a significant contribution.

## REFERENCES

Bishop, B. J. & Syme, G. J. (1992). Social change in rural settings: Lessons for community change agents. In D. Thomas & A. Veno (Eds.). *Psychology and social change* (pp. 93-lll). Palmerston North: The Dunmore Press, Ltd.

Dokecki, P. (1992). On knowing the community of caring persons: A methodological basis for the reflective generative practice of community psychology. *Journal of Community Psychology, 20,* 26–35.

Huygens, I. (1995). *Depowering the powerful-beyond empowerment: Community psychology's avoidance of world empowerment patterns.* Paper presented at the Fifth Biennial Conference on Community Research and Action, Chicago, U.S.A.

Newbrough, J.R. (1992). Community psychology in the postmodern world. *Journal of Community Psychology, 20,* 10–25.

Reinharz, S. (1994). Toward an Ethnography of 'Voice' and 'Silence.' In E. J. Trickett, R.J. Watts & D. Birman (Eds.), *Human diversity: Perspectives on people in context* (pp. 178-200). San Francisco: Jossey Bass.

Smith, K.K. (1983). A role for community psychologists: As participant conceptualizers. *Australian Psychologist, 18,* 143-160.

Wicker, A.W. (1989). Substantive theorizing. *American Journal of Community Psychology, 17,* 531-547.

Wicker, A.W. & Sommer, R. (1993). The resident researcher: An alternative career model centered on community. *American Journal of Community Psychology, 21,* 469–482.

# Research and Evaluation Consulting

## Susan M. Wolfe

The University of Texas at Dallas

**SUMMARY.** This article describes the training, skills, and experiences that have been helpful to me in my work as an independent research and evaluation consultant. It describes the classes and formal education, research and program evaluation skills, work-related experiences, and publications, presentations and grant writing experiences. It concludes with a brief description of the work I have done as a consultant and how it has affected my career plans following completion of my dissertation. *[Article copies available for a fee from The Haworth Document Delivery Service: 1-800-342-9678. E-mail address: getinfo@haworthpressinc.com <Website: http://haworthpressinc. com>]*

**KEYWORDS.** Program evaluation, consultation, community psychology

For the past three years I have been working part-time as an independent research and evaluation consultant while working to complete my doctorate. My graduate education has included near-completion of a Ph.D. program (ABD) in ecological psychology with a cognate in organizational psychology. I changed graduate programs for two reasons. The first, and primary, reason was that my husband's job transferred him to another state, and attempts at completing my dissertation long-distance were not successful. The second was that I had become interested in doing research on adolescents and needed a greater un-

---

Address correspondence to: Susan M. Wolfe, School of Human Development, University of Texas at Dallas, Box 830688 GR41, Richardson, TX 75083-0688.

[Haworth co-indexing entry note]: "Research and Evaluation Consulting." Wolfe, Susan M. Co-published simultaneously in *Journal of Prevention & Intervention in the Community* (The Haworth Press, Inc.) Vol. 19, No. 2, 2000, pp. 21-27; and: *Employment in Community Psychology: The Diversity of Opportunity* (ed: Clifford R. O'Donnell, and Joseph R. Ferrari) The Haworth Press, Inc., 2000, pp. 21-27. Single or multiple copies of this article are available for a fee from The Haworth Document Delivery Service [1-800-342-9678, 9:00 a.m. - 5:00 p.m. (EST). E-mail address: getinfo@haworthpressinc.com].

derstanding of developmental psychology in order to do work that has substance. I am currently working on my dissertation on the development of autonomy in adolescence in a developmental psychology program.

I have held several jobs since I began graduate school, such as: research coordinator at a medical center; research associate at a center doing research on innovation in industry; assistant director of research for a large community college district; project director for a federally-funded, longitudinal study of homelessness; and, director of research and development at a non-profit children's mental health clinic. Consistent with the wide variety of positions has been a widely varied research content.

I began consulting when my position as director of research at the mental health clinic was going to be cut. While I was at the clinic, I had spent time working with various agencies on collaborative projects and committees and let my skills and expertise become known throughout the community. While attending a multi-agency meeting to discuss the submission of a proposal for family preservation funds that were soon to become available, someone noted that there would be a need for a program evaluator. I mentioned that I would be available to do it in January and the committee agreed to write me into the grant.

Since beginning as a consultant, I have been contracted to evaluate two family support projects, serve as local evaluator for the federally-funded Healthy Start project, and to design and implement a research project to gather data for planning teen pregnancy prevention programs. In this article I discuss the knowledge, skills and experiences that have been useful to me in conducting research in the community and working as an independent consultant.

## CLASSES AND OTHER FORMAL EDUCATION

Having a broad knowledge base to draw upon has been very helpful. The ecological psychology program gave me community research skills, knowledge of how communities work and how to work in them, and program evaluation methods. My knowledge of organizational psychology has been useful for working with non-profit organizations to understand decision processes, aspects of organizational change and organizational politics. Developmental psychology has given me the knowledge to assess the developmental appropriateness of assessment tools and interventions, and to develop research projects that are more substantive. Although I would never recommend that anyone go through more than one Ph.D. program, taking courses in a variety of disciplines can be very useful, even going outside of the psychology department and taking extra courses beyond those required.

I have also worked to develop a good working knowledge and understanding of statistics. In addition to the required statistical courses I took a multivariate statistics course that was offered at another university. I also attended a workshop on structural equation modeling and got hands-on experience with this technique. Being proficient and comfortable with a variety of statistical techniques is especially helpful since I generally work alone.

## RESEARCH AND EVALUATION SKILLS

So far in my work with community research and grant-funded projects, there has been no opportunity to use experimental design. Most grant-funded programs have small budgets for evaluation, and do not provide sufficient resources for a full-scale research project. Designing research that will be useful with a limited amount of resources requires some creativity and knowledge of quantitative and qualitative methods. This includes knowing how to design or locate measures that are valid and reliable and how to collect data from multiple sources. Some of this I learned in formal courses, the rest through experience.

In my job at the medical center I learned to apply program evaluation methods and collected data through personal interviews, videotaped interactions, telephone interviews, and review of medical and program charts. While working in the industrial innovation setting, I learned how to administer surveys in the workplace, how to work as part of a project team, and how to use a computer-assisted telephone-interview tool. While at the community college I learned to conduct focus groups. As project director for a longitudinal study of homelessness I learned about stratified sampling techniques and how to track subjects that had no address or phone. Each job contributed a new set of useful skills to my repertoire.

Despite my range of experiences, I still take time to continue learning skills and methods. Last year I attended a workshop on empowerment evaluation. As local evaluator for the Dallas Healthy Start project, I was required to attend a workshop on how to use a logic modeling process to develop the evaluation. This year I took a workshop in the political economy department to learn more about doing research on non-profit organizations.

## ADDITIONAL WORK REALTED EXPERIENCES

My work experiences have given me more knowledge than just research and evaluation related skills. In my job at the medical center, I learned about how medical settings function and became familiar with medical terminology. This has been helpful when projects require me to interact with medical personnel or projects that require collection of medical data.

Having worked in different positions at different levels of organizations has provided me with the viewpoint of different members of non-profit organizations. As assistant director of research for the community college district I was in a middle management position, caught between the campus personnel who relied on me for data and the demands of a supervisor who was more concerned with pleasing his superiors at the district office. My job at the clinic involved developing research and intervention projects and seeking grant funding. It allowed me to get to know my current community, the significant players and politics and the non-profit social service agency personnel. Community research and evaluation is very political and I am frequently confronted with competing interests. I also served on the board of directors for the homeless shelter in my community and became familiar with the policy-making side of running an agency.

Perhaps one of the most important work experiences I had was that of project director for the homelessness study. My experiences included supervising staff and students, organizing the work plan and delegating duties, budget management, assisting with writing the grant proposal and reports, development of the measurement protocol and sampling plan, data management and analyses, and interacting with community agencies to gain access to research participants. I also spent some time in the field talking with homeless individuals.

## PUBLICATIONS AND PRESENTATIONS

I have had several experiences that taught me the importance of negotiating publication and presentation plans at the beginning of a project. Early in my graduate school career I made significant conceptual and other contributions on a number of research projects, but found that plans did not include my name on publications, or there were no plans to submit articles from some projects. The result was that the work I did in the first years of graduate school gained me valuable experience, but no publications or presentations.

A second experience came when I began as evaluator for the family support project. There was concern among community members about how I would present the members of their community to the outside world. Previous researchers had come in and studied African-American children and described their deficits. I have used a couple of strategies to gain trust within this community. The first was to collect data that included strengths as well as deficits. When I write reports they provide a more balanced view of the program participants. The second has been to include program staff members on presentations and papers, and to help them to prepare their own presentations about the project.

## GRANT WRITING

All of my positions have provided me with grant-writing experience. I began helping to collect relevant supporting literature and appropriate outcome measures, then went on to participate in teams that were writing proposals. Now my experience includes either working as part of a team to develop a proposal, or singularly writing proposals for funds from government sources (federal, state and local), corporations, foundations and service clubs. Some have been successful, some have not. Although I prefer not to write grants at all, sometimes it is necessary and it is definitely a skill anyone with community interests will need.

## MY WORK AS AN INDEPENDENT CONSULTANT

At the time of the writing of this article, I am the evaluator for two projects. The evaluations have allowed me to remain active in community psychology and to combine my different areas of expertise and experience into something that is useful to the communities in which I work. My evaluations have included collection of both process and outcome data, and I have used a wide variety of methods and measures.

Most important in guiding my work has been my community psychology background and orientation. Empowerment has been a continuing theme throughout my work, and I frequently look for ways to incorporate the needs and concerns of clients (from their perspectives, not mine) in my recommendations. One program recommendation that was implemented was the addition of a consumer advisory committee to the family support program. For another project, we allowed adolescents to act as experts to tell us what they like and do not like in programs, and what approaches can really make an impact. As a follow-up, I am working with a group of adolescents to publish a newsletter of the study results to be distributed throughout the community. They have decided which information will be most interesting and useful to other adolescents, and their selections are very different from what I would have included.

There are both benefits and drawbacks to working as an independent research and evaluation consultant. One benefit is that I am usually able to set my own work hours and select my projects (yes, I have turned some down). I can also set my fees (within a certain range) and determine how much I will be paid. Since I do a lot of my work at home, I avoid commuting and do not have to worry about what to wear to work on those days. I have a lot of control over my schedule and my work.

A major drawback is the fluctuation in income and the need to do some self-marketing. Another is that program staff sometimes do not understand the need to keep careful records or to build the evaluation and data collection into the program. Sometimes the program staff do not like the evaluation findings (particularly if the findings expose negative staff behaviors). Community agencies may not come through with data they have promised, or other carefully made plans can go awry. Overall, the positives generally outweigh the negatives.

Although I do not plan to pursue this as a permanent and full-time career, it has been very useful for earning additional income and keeping me active within the community. It also provides me with real world experiences and viewpoints that helped to inform my more theoretical dissertation proposal.

Upon completion of my dissertation I intend to pursue an academic career. My research plans include developing better prevention services for adolescents. Working in the community with service providers has made me aware of the need for the kind of expertise that can be provided by someone with an academic background and an understanding of the ins-and-outs of providing services. In addition to developing my own prevention programs, I intend to continue to work with community-based organizations to help guide their program development and to design and implement good program evaluations.

Two community psychology principles that I learned in my first year of graduate school have been especially helpful in guiding my work. First, programs work best if they foster social support and provide individuals with stronger community connections. Second, programs must empower the recipients to take ownership of their problems and be active participants in the solutions; after all, they are the real experts.

# Education and Employment in Rural Alaska

## Carol Yakish

University of Alaska-Fairbanks

**SUMMARY.** The history of my work experience in rural Alaska suggests the value of combining academic and field experience in community psychology with employment in graduate school. Twelve years of employment in rural Alaska leading to my present position with a rural Alaska Native Health organization is briefly reviewed. It is concluded that graduate students should examine, carefully and openly, their choices in preparing a path for applied community psychology employment. *[Article copies available for a fee from The Haworth Document Delivery Service: 1-800-342-9678. E-mail address: getinfo@haworthpressinc.com <Website: http://www.haworthpressinc.com>]*

**KEYWORDS.** Cultural psychology, community psychology

For a period of four years I have been employed as an itinerant Social Worker for a regional Native nonprofit health corporation on the island of Kodiak in the Gulf of Alaska. Having lived on the island for the past twelve years, the idea of delivering services to remote village communities was not a new one to me, but it was challenging and offered the chance to glean from the local Native residents the proper and effective way in which my experience and education could augment the traditional and cultural lifestyle in these communities. The question I asked myself at the beginning of my employment was could I be effective in my ability to assimilate my *limited* knowledge

Address correspondence to: Carol Yakish, Department of Psychology, University of Alaska, Fairbanks, AK 99775.

[Haworth co-indexing entry note]: "Education and Employment in Rural Alaska." Yakish, Carol. Co-published simultaneously in *Journal of Prevention & Intervention in the Community* (The Haworth Press, Inc.) Vol. 19, No. 2, 2000, pp. 29-32; and: *Employment in Community Psychology: The Diversity of Opportunity* (ed: Clifford R. O'Donnell, and Joseph R. Ferrari) The Haworth Press, Inc., 2000, pp. 29-32. Single or multiple copies of this article are available for a fee from The Haworth Document Delivery Service [1-800-342-9678, 9:00 a.m. - 5:00 p.m. (EST). E-mail address: getinfo@haworthpressinc.com].

of intervention with the knowledge of culture and tradition character-
ized by the Aleut residents for whom I worked?

Kodiak is an island of approximately 14,000 people, with the majority of people living in the small city of Kodiak. The city's population hovers around 7,500 with expansion during the seasonal commercial fishing seasons. The six remote Native villages are only accessible
by boat and small plane. Their approximate populations range from 68
in Karluk to 300 in Old Harbor. The village community residents are
predominately Alaskan Natives. All have organized tribal councils as
well as city councils. Finding a niche in this remote island milieu was
not difficult. It offers all that I consider necessary, and what is missing
is cultivated by the people, community connectedness (Elias, 1987)
and solidarity one finds in such "tight knit" surroundings.

The attractiveness of being able to travel to remote villages and do
direct service work was the draw that prompted me to apply for the
position of Social Worker. The work would be broad in scope, offering
a variety of grant programs in which to be involved and make contributions to the village communities. Since I believed in sovereignty,
Alaskan Native rights and preservation of the Native village tradition,
I felt enthusiastic and honored to be a non-Native among those serving
these rural communities. I would be addressing social/economic issues
that had a footing in generational transition thousands of years old. At
the time, it did not appear to be a formidable task.

My knowledge of a rural Native community was awakened from a
narrow, romantic view of Alaskan Native life to the reality of a macro-
cosm of indigenous life tinged with western influences that had brought
numerous negative as well as a few positive changes to a once simple
and complete subsistence lifestyle. I saw the decline of prosperity and
the ascension of social problems and ills. The rural definitions of these
problems were concurrent with the urban communities' problems, but
the *effect and affect* they extended to the rural community members was
monumental in proportion to the urban community. When an individual
in a rural village experienced a crisis or problem there was the likelihood that the *entire* community would be affected in some way. Being
able to relate and work with the community on their terms, with their
needs as the focus is the challenge to a community psychologist.

In a needs assessment of rural Native villages conducted in 1995 in
Native villages throughout Alaska, Cunningham (1995) found that the
Kodiak village families and key village service providers identified
important local interpretation of the severity of problems experienced

by families within their communities. The outcomes reflect the following prioritization: (1) substance abuse; (2) juvenile crime; (3) child abuse; (4) teen pregnancy; (5) mental health; (6) physical health, and (8) basic needs. The responses of key informants (local village service providers) ranked the severity of problems experienced by families as follows: (1) substance abuse; (2) domestic violence; (3) juvenile crime; (4) teen pregnancy; (5/6 tie) child abuse and mental health; (7) physical health, and (8) basic needs.

The problems as ranked by each of the two groups indicates the exposure and reaction to areas of concern in rural environments as being much the same as experienced in urban environments. I found through my position's contact within these communities that the intensity of concern and hope for a safer, healthier environment for families and children was absolute even if the path was uncertain. My longing for a new view of how I might better serve the needs and shortages of resources for my villages was perpetuated by the visual and human context these tables gave to my scope of work. I needed more effective and innovative ways of helping communities positively impact their path to wellness.

After the third year in my current position, I was accepted into the graduate "Community Psychology" Program at the University of Alaska, Fairbanks, which now offered a distance education program. This allowed the student to remain working in their community while attending classes via teleconferencing and two week intensive on-campus sessions throughout the two year program. A perfect answer to my growing need to educate and re-educate myself and my thinking of social service delivery. The graduate program in community psychology would begin with courses in community psychology, counseling, methods of assessment, psychological assessment and field-based research. The emphasis would be in delivery of culturally relevant and appropriate practices in rural Alaska. The knowledge-base I had in entering the program would be intently challenged and changed by the dawning of this experience. In this first year of the program, I am learning to re-evaluate the basic principles that guided my perception of prevention, empowerment, advocacy and self-help to this point in my career.

Working full-time and attending graduate school full-time has proven to be an asset in my new endeavor. What I am learning, sharing and experiencing with fellow students is exciting, thought-provoking, and inspiring. I am finding new respect and enthusiasm for my job. I am also finding the opportunity to promote change and prevention in a new and empowering way. I am learning that for a primary prevention program to be effective it must, by design, present empowerment to its components. Through this dissemination of constructural empowerment, the inhabitants of a community, by their willingness and motivation to participate, will enhance their own competencies and self-worth. I could be a part of impacting the empowerment of rural Alaska.

The ecological impact of community psychology and intervention depends on whether or not the feelings of empowerment, connectedness, and relatedness (Elias, 1987) will take hold or whether the intervention is merely a process of power by a non-connected entity. In other words, does the intervention reflect the community in which it is being carried out? I believe that meaningful intervention in a rural setting must be environmentally-based with the community inhabitants as one of its essential components. Once this component is established, the response to the intervention by its participants and the makeup of the environment in which it is presented will all interact and enhance the *connectedness* which the intervention strives to achieve. As a community psychologist in rural Alaska, one can help initiate Native community empowerment.

As I interact with my village communities and residents, I further my understanding of how community psychology can and will be helpful in my current and future positions. For some, I recommend combining the academic and field experience with employment even with the hardships and allowances required of such an endeavor. For others, a more defined and separate choice may be the answer. Whatever the choice, with a clear understanding of purpose and final expectation in either course, one can strengthen a track that will benefit the employed student as well as their employing agency or business. As for my own employment future and plans after graduation, I expect to continue within the area of primary prevention and clinical treatment of child sexual and physical abuse in rural Alaska.

## REFERENCES

Cunningham, Patrick M. (1995). Supporting and Preserving Alaska's Families, Our Finest Resource. *Family Preservation and Support Needs Assessment.* 226.

Elias, Maurice J. (1987). Establishing Enduring Prevention Programs: Advancing the Legacy of Swampscott, *American Journal of Community Psychology 15*(5), 539–551.

Maton, K., & Salem, D. (1995). Organizational Characteristics of Empowering Community Settings: A Multiple Case Study Approach, *American Journal of Community Psychology 23*(5), 631–656.

Trickett, Edison J. (1997). Ecology and Primary prevention: Reflections on a Meta-Analysis, *American Journal of Community Psychology 25*(2), 197–205.

# Practicing What We Preach: Integrating Community Psychology into the Job Search Process

Rebecca Campbell

Department of Psychology
University of Illinois at Chicago

Holly Angelique

Department of Behavioral Sciences and Education
Pennsylvania State University at Harrisburg

Bonnie J. BootsMiller

University of Michigan Substance Abuse Research Center
Ann Arbor VA Medical Center

William S. Davidson II

Department of Psychology
Michigan State University

**SUMMARY.** This paper describes the creation of a "Job Club" at Michigan State University to facilitate employment searches in Community Psychology. The goal of the Job Club was to provide a setting where graduating Ph.D. candidates could gain the skills necessary to be

---

Address correspondence to: Rebecca Campbell, Department of Psychology (M/C 285), University of Illinois at Chicago, 1007 West Harrison, Chicago, IL 60607-7137 (e-mail: rmc@uic.edu).

[Haworth co-indexing entry note]: "Practicing What We Preach: Integrating Community Psychology into the Job Search Process." Campbell et al. Co-published simultaneously in *Journal of Prevention & Intervention in the Community* (The Haworth Press, Inc.) Vol. 19, No. 2, 2000, pp. 33-43; and: *Employment in Community Psychology: The Diversity of Opportunity* (ed: Clifford R. O'Donnell, and Joseph R. Ferrari) The Haworth Press, Inc., 2000, pp. 33-43. Single or multiple copies of this article are available for a fee from The Haworth Document Delivery Service [1-800-342-9678, 9:00 a.m. - 5:00 p.m. (EST). E-mail address: getinfo@haworthpressinc.com].

successful in both academic and non-academic job searches. The Job Club was student-driven, and emphasized principles of community psychology such as collaboration, network development, social and instrumental support, and empowerment. The importance of small group size and the ongoing commitment of a senior faculty mentor are highlighted. A curriculum for Job Club was created that included: re- source allocation; network development; document development (vitae, resumes); practicing job talks, teaching demonstrations and interviews; and accepting the offer. Successes, lessons learned, and suggestions for creating Job Clubs in other settings are offered. *[Article copies available for a fee from The Haworth Document Delivery Service: 1-800-342-9678. E-mail address: getinfo@haworthpressinc.com <Website: http://haworthpressinc.com>]*

**KEYWORDS.** Community psychology, job club, employment, em- powerment

Completing a dissertation and beginning a job search is unnerving, and many graduate students have felt alone and alienated in this pro- cess. Unfortunately, many graduate programs have overlooked this critical aspect of graduate training. In an effort to empower ourselves, a group of graduate students, along with a faculty mentor, decided to put the principles of community psychology into practice and created The Job Club. In the Fall of 1995, a group of four graduate students and one faculty member in ecological-community psychology at Michigan State University convened to discuss employment options in community psychology. All four students were entering the job mar- ket: two seeking academic jobs, two seeking non-academic positions. The task before the faculty advisor was to mentor four very different people through the process of obtaining employment in the field of community psychology. Within this context, we decided to meet regu- larly (once every two weeks throughout the fall and every week in the winter), provide support and feedback to each other, and share re- sources in our search for jobs. In this paper, we will describe the curriculum of Job Club from the perspective of the club members (the students), and examine how this program integrated key concepts of community psychology, such as fostering empowerment, bolstering social support, and creating resources.

## DEVELOPMENT OF GROUND RULES

In an initial meeting of the Job Club, all members acknowledged that searching for employment was extremely stressful, so a group commitment was made to a spirit of support and collaboration, rather than one of competition. A primary source of potential conflict was overlapping employment interests. To confront this issue, boundaries were set between the academic and non-academic positions, geographic preferences, content areas of expertise, and type of job (e.g., primarily research-oriented versus teaching-oriented). In discussing these differences it became evident that only a few areas of overlap were problematic. With a continued spirit of cooperation, the group discussed whether multiple group members would apply for the same job or whether a trade-off strategy should be adopted. The prevailing wisdom was that a trade-off strategy would be potentially more rewarding, especially since all group members were relying on letters of reference from some of the same faculty members. The group agreed that a reference letter written for the individual "best" suited for a particular job would be diluted by an additional letter from the same referee for another job candidate. The group decided that in instances of overlap, the individuals with overlapping interests would meet separately to discuss their interests and decide which employment positions were better suited to each individual. In the end, these overlap issues were extremely minimal, with positions being easily divided when the individuals met to discuss their overlapping interests. However, the importance of these procedures for the prevention of conflict should not be underestimated.

The resolution of these issues contributed to the strength and cooperative philosophy of the group. The continuing functions of the Job Club were to gather resources and learn the skills necessary in finding and obtaining a position. A curriculum was developed to provide knowledge and skill acquisition in job search strategies, writing a strong vitae/resume, preparing and practicing for interviews, talks, and demonstration, and negotiating the offer.

## THE JOB CLUB CURRICULUM

Nine topics were covered in our Job Club curriculum. For each of the topics explored, we examined how they would apply for both academic and non-academic positions. Given that the members of the group had recently spent many years of training and socialization in an academic setting, many meetings emphasized academic positions in more detail than non-academic settings. To the extent possible, we

attempted to provide equal attention to these two routes of employment. Following is a loose chronology of the topics covered.

*Gathering Resources.* The first topic covered in the Job Club curriculum was gathering the necessary resources to begin an employment
search. All members of the group were assigned to bring different
publications with job listings, and to search for other articles about the
job search process. Among the resources gathered: the *APA Monitor*,
the *APS Observer*, the *Chronicle of Higher Education*, Professional
newsletters (e.g., *The Community Psychologist*), local and regional
newspapers, employment bulletins published by the state of Michigan,
and email announcements. Job openings discovered by "word-of-
mouth" were also discussed. Articles and books about the job search
process were shared (e.g., Zanna and Darley's (1987) *The Compleat
Academic*). In reviewing these materials, we found useful leads and
opportunities for both academic and non-academic positions (e.g.,
non-academic jobs advertised in the *APA Monitor*).

*Network Development.* To find a job, it is important that key people
in your target employment settings know you're looking for a job.
Several of our early Job Club meetings focused on developing a network of contacts. Although this is important for both academic and
non-academic searches, it was particularly important for those working in community settings to be well-connected. To assess the strength
of our networks, we were all asked to bring our "rolodex of contacts"–who we had worked with before, who we knew, who we had
met before, and who those people knew. In sharing our contacts, our
networks grew substantially just from this initial discussion. To build
new contacts, we discussed ways to meet new people and inform them
of a job search: making initial phone contact, requesting lunch meetings, providing a short summary of your work and skills (the "sound-
bite"), and presenting your resume or vita with a request to pass it
along to others who might be interested in your work.

*Vita and Resume Development.* A single advertised position can
elicit hundreds of applications, so a strong vita and/or resume is essential to catch the attention of search committees and potential employers. Therefore, developing vitae and resumes was the focus of several
meetings. Although the curriculum vitae (a listing of all major work
accomplished throughout one's career) is more common in academic
settings, and resumes (a summary listing of highlights from one's
career) more in non-academic settings, all of us were encouraged to

develop both versions. We collected the vitae and resumes of recent graduates of our program and recent hires made by our program to serve as models. We discussed, page by page, section by section, what should be included in these documents, such as: name, address, and contact information; list of research interests; list of teaching interests; education; employment; publications; conference presentations; consulting and community experience; grants; other professional service; and references. Depending on the job focus, these topics would be covered in varying orders and varying degrees. For example, in non-academic jobs, publications might be listed toward the end of the document; for academic jobs, they would begin on the first page, if possible. Our "homework" assignment was to develop our vitae and/ or resumes and bring multiple copies to the group for feedback. These discussions were invaluable in shaping the development of these documents as our peers could see our work with a unique and fresh perspective, which helped each of us to highlight our strengths. Once we had established a solid "baseline" vita and resume, we discussed ways in which multiple versions should be created that would be more tailored to the specific jobs for which we would be applying.

*Other Documents to Be Developed.* With our vitae and resumes developed, we moved on to discuss how to prepare many of the other documents that are requested in the job search process: cover letters, statement of research interests, statement of teaching interests and philosophy, course syllabi and course evaluations, submitted grant applications, executive summary reports from consultation projects, and academic transcripts. Following the process we used to develop our vitae and resumes, we each drafted the other documents appropriate for our job search and brought them to the group for feedback. As a result, our application packages were much improved. By defining ourselves as stronger candidates, we "became" stronger candidates.

*The Job Search Process.* What positions should we apply for? What are we trained to do? Over the course of our Job Club meetings, we began to realize that our vision of our skills was far too narrow. Initially, if a position did not explicitly state "community psychologist wanted," we were inclined to move on to the next listing. To learn more about the search process, we each reviewed the job listings we had obtained in the first part of the Job Club curriculum and gathered all the job announcements for which we felt qualified. These lists were shared with the group, and invariably were met with comments such as, "What about this one? Why didn't you consider this? You can do this." Just as when we were developing our vitae and resumes, we realized that our peers could often see our work in a different, and often more encouraging, light. As a result, our search lists grew, and we applied for a wider range of jobs–those that seemed "perfect fits" and those that seemed to be more of a stretch. Throughout this process it was important to remember that what a position looked like on paper did not always reflect what it might be like in real life. The "perfect fits" may be "perfect misses," and the "seems like a stretch" could in reality be the perfectly tailored position.

The success of this stage of the process was largely attributed to our pre-existing ground rules. Because the strategy for approaching overlapping interests was already decided, our spirit of cooperation grew. At this point, we had accumulated many resources and realized that we were far more qualified than we originally believed. This helped us to overcome the myth of limited opportunity. Our training in community psychology had equipped us with many tools and skills that we could take with us into our careers. Additionally, we had become empowered to consider the multiple opportunities for which we were qualified.

*The Job Talk.* We initially thought that only those applying for academic jobs would need to prepare a presentation of their work, but we found that some recent graduates of our program who worked in non-academic settings had been asked to provide a brief presentation of their work. Consequently, we were all encouraged to develop a presentation of our research. Key suggestions we followed in the development of these presentations included: (1) to develop a clear organization of the talk and to present a general outline or overview to your audience at the beginning of the talk; (2) to speak in a language that is accessible to multiple groups: imagine how your talk would sound to someone in a different field within psychology or a different discipline; (3) to use clear, easy-to-read overheads to summarize key points; and (4) to keep the introductory material brief to leave plenty of time for the actual presentation of your research. We practiced our talks in Job Club, asking for feedback in both content and presentation style (e.g., "Did you know that you cross your arms tightly across your body when someone asks you a question?"). We then practiced our talks again in a larger group where we had specifically invited people from different disciplines within the department to assess how our work was perceived by others. The overarching message at this stage of the process was to "practice, practice, practice." Once again, our work paid off and our presentations became stronger.

*Teaching Demonstrations.* Those applying for academic positions also prepared a sample teaching demonstration. As in our preparation of the job talk, we discussed how to make this presentation well-organized and understandable to different audiences. These presentations were also practiced in Job Club, and then again in a more diverse audience.

*Job Interview.* Obtaining an interview may seem difficult enough, but "delivering" a successful interview is the key to getting the job. The details of the interview process are critical because collegiality and personality may be as important to your potential employer as your qualifications. Therefore, planning for a job interview was discussed over several weeks. First, we explored ways to learn more about the department or agencies with whom we would be interviewing (e.g., searching the internet; learning faculty names and research interests; reviewing the agency organizational chart). Second, we developed lists of questions to ask at our interviews (e.g., what to ask the faculty, students, department chair, and dean; what to ask the other members of the agency's team, the executive director, the board of directors). Third, we walked through how to prepare a start-up budget and/or list of other resources needed to begin a position (e.g., salary negotiations, computers, software, support staff, office supplies, books, journals). Fourth, we practiced how to describe our research interests and our plans for future work in clear, concise "sound-bites." Fifth, we discussed how to approach the "social interactions" on interview day (e.g., appropriate humor, what to eat at lunch/dinner [no garlic, nothing messy, whether it is acceptable to drink alcohol]). Finally, we discussed some of the smaller, yet still stressful, details, such as what to wear and packing tips (e.g., don't put the notes for your talk in your luggage and then check your luggage with the airlines). To integrate this material about interviewing, we conducted mock interviews and role-played different situations in the interview process (e.g., "I'm the chair of the department or division leader at the agency, and I've just asked you what kind of salary you're looking for. . ."). These seemingly minor details helped tremendously during the actual interviews. Carrying a list of questions to ask in a pocket or briefcase was invaluable, facilitating intelligent inquiry rather than the "I can't think of anything to ask" feeling that can come with anxiety.

*Closing the Deal and Making the Transition to Employment.* As we returned from our interviews, we continued to meet to discuss the final negotiations in accepting an offer (salary, benefits, teaching load, moving expenses, start dates). Our Job Club was successful and all members received offers from our first job interviews, and all turned out to be where we eventually accepted. After accepting the offers, we met occasionally to discuss how to prepare for starting our new positions.

## PRACTICING WHAT WE PREACH: INTEGRATING COMMUNITY PSYCHOLOGY INTO THE JOB SEARCH PROCESS

We believe that the success of the Job Club was because we integrated key concepts of community psychology into our job search process. The Job Club provided a collective, collaborative structure for the usually competitive process of job searching. The skills we learned and practiced in Job Club improved our marketability, but in creating this program, we also had the opportunity to transcend the alienation and disempowerment that usually accompanies this process.

First, collaboration and network development were considered cornerstones of our Job Club's success. Building upon a philosophy of collaboration allowed us to ward off many potential conflicts before any might escalate. It provided a setting where ground rules could be established and gave us all an initial sense of unity with each other and control over our group process. From this location, we were able to develop our networks outside of the group and felt positive about sharing the information we gathered with the group.

Second, the social support provided among the members of Job Club was invaluable. We had other people to talk with who were under similar stresses, and the support and encouragement provided by the group was a key factor in building our confidence for our job interviews. No one in the group had to go through the search process alone. Rather than competing for "perceived" limited job opportunities in our field, we felt as though we were all in this together. We worked as a group in every task, from learning how to build a vita, to shopping for interview clothes, to helping each other relax the day before interviews, and to celebrate in the successful job offer. Just having someone to call after a stressful day of interviewing in an unfamiliar city, and knowing that person would understand your situation made the interview process more friendly.

*The support was also instrumental.* Job Club enhanced our skills in consultation and feedback. We learned more about how to provide constructive feedback, and receive feedback, throughout the process of creating our vitae, searching for jobs, and preparing for interviews. Through this feedback, we gained a better appreciation of our strengths and competencies. These skills have transferred to our current positions, both academic and non-academic, where feedback and critique are required often.

Third, Job Club was an empowering setting for addressing this very stressful life transition. Approaching the completion of the dissertation may leave many graduate students feeling ill-prepared to leave the role of a graduate student and to transition into the role of professional in the field. Graduate school provides a safety net of sorts, including a network of advisors and mentors, funding opportunities, and sometimes even housing and relief from student loans. The prospect of leaving may feel like being "kicked out of the nest" before we are ready. This feeling may be exacerbated by the often alienating and disempowering process of completing the dissertation itself. Feeling alone and unprepared, a job candidate in this state may approach the job search and interview from a perspective of low self-esteem and limited qualifications. The Job Club was similar to a self-help group. The members supported each other and created an ongoing, informal network of support. Together, we came to a new understanding of our many strengths and were able to present ourselves to potential employers from a perspective of competence and self-efficacy. With a spirit of collaboration, our peers were able to provide constructive feedback on our work, and allow us to see our skills and potential. Individually, and as a group, we became empowered.

Finally, the sense of empowerment instilled by Job Club and the skills and strategies acquired did not end when the members left to fulfill their prospective positions. Review of the nine principles in the Job Club curriculum has provided a good refresher course for one of the Job Club members who entered a post-doctoral fellowship and is currently using the principles and procedures to search for a permanent position. Although group support is now long-distance, she has a firm understanding of the necessary ingredients to maximize her job searching efforts.

## LESSONS LEARNED

Upon reflection, the success of the group may be attributed, in part, to a small group size and the ongoing, active involvement of a senior faculty mentor. A group of four was advantageous because we could plan schedules to attend practice talks. Even though we were stretched to our own limits with job preparations, we could find time to review each others' work without be overwhelmed with multiple documents. Our faculty mentor kept us on task, provided much insight into the job search, and was truly committed to successfully placing us into appropriate careers.

Establishing initial ground rules was essential to our success. In our case, the diverse interests of the group members alleviated potential conflict from the onset. However, we did not dismiss or deny potential conflict as an issue to be addressed when needed. The old adage that "if it ain't broke, don't fix it" did not apply here. We did identify overlapping interests, such as Women's Studies minors, that may have led multiple individuals to the same job. Only by specifically and deliberately addressing such issues early were conflicts avoided later. With unresolved conflict, group cohesion would have quickly deteriorated. Careful planning provided the foundation for positive experiences.

In the process of applying for jobs and interviewing, we learned that our training and skills had provided a foundation for success in many employment settings. With a little network development, unlimited positions for community psychologists seemed to exist. Although we were all trained in ecological-community psychology, we had different strengths and interests (developmental psychology, criminal justice, women's studies, program evaluation, mental health services). We came to understand that there are a variety of settings in which community psychologists are employable, and that we each fit best in different settings. Rather than viewing the field as small and limited, we came to see community psychology as growing and expansive. Perhaps one of the greatest successes of the group came from our collective ability to overcome a fear of limited opportunity that could have led to competition and conflict.

When we decided to create a Job Club to facilitate our job searches in Community Psychology, it may be fair to say that fear and trepidation were among our collective feelings. Some of us had witnessed friendships deteriorate and hostility bloom as a result of the competitive nature of the job market. We were all very busy and could not possibly imagine finding time to help other people with their employment searches. However, we also saw the potential of such a group. We were feeling isolated in our struggles to complete our doctorates and realized that involvement could be personally and collectively beneficial. The Job Club could be student-driven–we could create a setting that would work for us. We wanted to practice the principles of community psychology in our personal and professional lives. This seemed like one way to combine the personal and the professional, while practicing what we so often preach about collaboration, networking, social support and empowerment.

## REFERENCE

Zanna, M.P., & Darley, J.M. (1987). *The compleat academic: A practical guide for the beginning social scientist.* New York: McGraw Hill.

# Community Psychology Graduate Employment in Aotearoa New Zealand

Kathryn Nemec
Ruth Hungerford
Linda Hutchings
Ingrid Huygens

University of Waikato

**SUMMARY.** Employment experiences of graduates from the community psychology program in New Zealand are explored. Thirty-eight of the total number of 45 graduates from the program were interviewed. A brief description of work settings, relevance of community psychology training for obtaining employment, and the practice of community psychology concepts in the workplace provide the context for two case studies. *[Article copies available for a fee from The Haworth Document Delivery Service: 1-800-342-9678. E-mail address: getinfo@haworthpressinc.com <Website: http://www.haworthpressinc.com>]*

**KEYWORDS.** Community psychology, employment

## INTRODUCTION

The Department of Psychology at the University of Waikato offers the only training program for community psychologists in New Zea-

---

Address correspondence to; Kathryn Nemec, 9a Kingsley Street, Westmere, Auckland, New Zealand.

[Haworth co-indexing entry note]: "Community Psychology Graduate Employment in Aotearoa New Zealand." Nemec et al. Co-published simultaneously in *Journal of Prevention & Intervention in the Community* (The Haworth Press, Inc.) Vol. 19, No. 2, 2000, pp. 45-52; and: *Employment in Community Psychology: The Diversity of Opportunity* (ed: Clifford R. O'Donnell, and Joseph R. Ferrari) The Haworth Press, Inc., 2000, pp. 45-52. Single or multiple copies of this article are available for a fee from The Haworth Document Delivery Service [1-800-342-9678, 9:00 a.m. - 5:00 p.m. (EST). E-mail address: getinfo@haworthpressinc.com].

*45*

land. Graduates of the three-year program receive a Master of Social Science degree and a post-graduate Diploma in Psychology (Community), and are eligible to register as psychologists. The Diploma involves four skills based courses in community psychology practice plus a year long internship.

The program commenced in 1980, with the first students graduating in 1983. The yearly intake is restricted, with a maximum of six students accepted. To date, 45 students have graduated from the program. In order to gather information about their career paths and the relevance of their community psychology training to their employment, 38 graduates were interviewed by phone (7 were unable to be contacted).

Of the 38 graduates (28 women, 10 men), 7 had only one job since graduating (6 of whom had graduated only one year ago and the seventh, three years ago) while the majority had between two and eight jobs. Most graduates spent an average of one to three years in one job and some 'juggled' two or more part-time jobs or contracts at the same time.

The government sector was the most common employer, with graduates mostly working in the health and local government area. Self-employment, particularly in the education and research area, was the next most popular option, followed by working for non-governmental/ charitable organizations, and private sector organizations. Three graduates had completed or were completing PhDs and one, a research fellowship.

A wide variety of job titles were reported by graduates including Corporate Planner, Community Development Officer, Injury Prevention Consultant, General Manager (Mental Health), Mediator, and Senior Health Analyst. Only one respondent had an official job title of Community Psychologist. Research and evaluation, followed by counseling and mediation, emerged as the main tasks undertaken by community psychology graduates in their careers to date. It should be noted that counseling and mediation was mostly done alongside primary tasks, such as human resource consultancy and health promotion.

## RELEVANCE OF COMMUNITY PSYCHOLOGY TRAINING FOR OBTAINING EMPLOYMENT

Community psychology graduates mostly considered that the training had assisted them to obtain employment, although some had been disappointed in the relevance of the training to future employment. Among the skills considered most useful for obtaining employment were applied and empirical social research skills, especially evaluation research. As one graduate commented: *"Evaluation research is a meal ticket and my most marketable skill."*

Graduates also reported that the community psychology training provided a framework and vocabulary with which to articulate values they may already have held. Such a framework assisted with obtaining employment, as one graduate commented: *"They liked my understanding of social systems and the political aspects of human dysfunction, for example, patriarchy and racism."*

From the comments made by respondents, it would appear that prospective employers are not necessarily looking to employ a community psychology graduate. Certainly, no jobs are advertised for community psychologists, and there is virtually no understanding of community psychology as a profession amongst employers. However, in the interview process employers seemed to appreciate the ideas and values espoused by a community psychologist. In this sense, the philosophy and values of community psychology are relevant to obtaining employment, and to ensuring an appropriate match between the graduate and prospective employment.

However, many graduates gave credit to other factors in obtaining employment such as the post-graduate nature of the qualification, previous work experience, training in areas such as counseling and facilitation, and breadth of previous organizational experience.

## UNIQUENESS OF COMMUNITY PSYCHOLOGY TRAINING IN THE EYES OF AN EMPLOYER

Graduates mostly believed that their employers could have appointed someone from another professional training background. Only a few felt that their employers would have considered someone solely from their particular background. The other professional training that employers could have considered included: anyone with social science skills or a background in any social science area, market research or general qualitative research skills, and anyone with a human resource, health, or counseling background.

The recognition obtained from a master's level and post-graduate qualification was considered beneficial for obtaining employment. For some respondents, particularly those working as a 'psychologist,' the ability to register as a psychologist was very important.

## *KEY SKILLS*
## *THAT DISTINGUISH COMMUNITY PSYCHOLOGISTS*
## *IN THEIR PRESENT POSITIONS*

In contrast to their beliefs about the "employers' eye view," approximately three quarters of the graduates (26) felt that they did in fact have key skills that enabled them to perform their job better than someone from another professional background. In the graduate's view, their postgraduate qualification gave them a high level of academic expertise, including writing and oral skills useful in report writing and presentations. In addition, the diploma taught or validated a range of interpersonal and research skills, such as interviewing, consultation, facilitation, and empirical and statistical research processes. Graduates perceived that other professions did not provide this range or breadth of skills.

There were specific approaches taught in community psychology that graduates felt gave them an edge over other professions. The interdisciplinary, multi-level approach allowed graduates to work with all levels of an organization, and from a variety of internal and external perspectives. *"We can work up and down, in and out," "We have the ability to take individual, community, organizational, or cultural/ societal perspectives and to link all these"* and *"[we have] . . . the structural analysis approach."*

The focus on community, culture and society taught in community psychology provided a collective approach to research and interventions for a number of graduates. Furthermore, graduates noted that they were generalists, able to find their own solutions, and to make recommendations or develop policy from research.

## *RELEVANCE OF COMMUNITY PSYCHOLOGY CONCEPTS*
## *IN THE WORKPLACE*

Almost all graduates noted that a range of community psychology concepts, such as *empowerment, advocacy,* and *participation,* were important in their workplaces. However, not all respondents reported that these concepts were reinforced in their workplace, either due to doing work that did not utilize these concepts, or because they were considered unimportant to the organization. One explanation may be that whilst community psychology concepts were important at an individual and team level, they may be contradicted in the overall organization culture, including within the university environment.

## CASE STUDIES
## OF COMMUNITY PSYCHOLOGY GRADUATES

The following case studies illustrate the career paths and experiences of two community psychology graduates.

*Case Study 1*: The first case study highlights the employment diversity of a community psychology graduate. Like most graduates, she has had a high number of jobs, with seven different employers in nine years. She has worked as a coordinator of alcohol and drug services, a researcher for the Human Rights Commission, a volunteer doing bicultural education and anti-racism work with Pakeha (European-derived settlers in Aotearoa, New Zealand), an injury rehabilitation coordinator, a community developer for local government, and is currently a community relations manager for the national Health Funding Authority. Two of the key roles of her current job are communication, which involves informing the community about health services and funding decisions, and advocacy, ensuring they have a voice in decisions regarding the purchase of health services.

The diversity of her experience and community networks developed over years of community-oriented work helped obtain her current position. However, she considered that there were also aspects of the community psychology training that made her suitable for the position, in particular the theoretical approach and research skills taught in the program. In terms of values, she noted that as a feminist she had a political analysis and values compatible with community psychology, prior to enrolling in the program. However, the program built on these, giving her the skills and deeper level of analysis to address complex problems in a disciplined and research oriented manner. The skills she acquired in structural analysis, evaluation, needs assessment, and collecting and analyzing qualitative data have been invaluable.

Interestingly, she noted that in her organization, employers do not regard community psychology training as particularly relevant. Indeed, explaining community psychology is difficult, and the key concepts, such as empowerment, advocacy and participation are considered dated (80s) and ill defined. In order to gain a new language to describe these concepts and make them relevant to the business environment of the health sector in Aotearoa New Zealand, she completed a Diploma of Business, specializing in Human Resource Management.

*Case Study 2*: The second case study highlights the need to acknowledge that for those who already observe or practice values consistent with community psychology, the university training may have limited usefulness. In fact, a community psychology course may serve to colonise or invalidate such values or philosophy by its lack of recognition of other knowledge systems. In this case, an indigenous graduate struggled to defend the validity of kaupapa Maori (Maori systems of knowledge and practice) approaches and practice during her training. She learned, in fact, that community psychology tools and concepts were often new names for existing phenomena in kaupapa Maori.

Advocacy, for instance, is essential to the activities of a Maori person in many roles, since it is a duty to better the position of one's people. In kaupapa Maori practice, this concept and duty is not exclusive to community psychology work, or even to health or social welfare work.

The empowerment concept as used in community psychology is based on assumptions that the community psychologist has certain power in the first place. In contrast, the Maori concept of tino rangatiratanga or 'absolute authority' is based in the world view that power is vested in each local group of people. The notion of a visitor 'empowering' a local group does not make sense in such a system. She rejected the attempt by community psychology to claim ownership of concepts that are basic to Maori thinking.

Since graduating, she has held four positions, working as an evaluation researcher, policy analyst, coordinator of a national prevention programme, and self employed consultant. In each position, she has focused on Maori needs. She is currently engaged in doctoral research on Maori smoking cessation, using a kaupapa Maori theoretical framework.

She acknowledged that she gained limited professional benefits from the community psychology course, naming evaluation research skills as most valuable, in particular Patton's utilisation focused approach. In contrast to her colleagues in public health and health promotion who limited themselves to descriptive or epidemiological reports, she followed the utilization approach whereby it is the role of the evaluation researcher to use several layers of analysis, and make recommendations and suggestions. She also felt that her psychological training had given her an edge in understanding the complexity of human behavior, including moving between a Maori and a Western model.

She pointed out, however, that in her recent research work she has returned to a basic psychology research design. She feels that the community aspect of her degree has been largely irrelevant to her employment. Most important has been that she is Maori and highly qualified, with the title 'psychologist.'

## CONCLUSIONS

Graduates were employed in a range of jobs and roles and reported undertaking a variety of key tasks in their various positions. The most frequently reported tasks were evaluation research and counseling.

Most graduates felt that their community psychology training had helped them obtain their present positions, either with an employer or as self-employed workers. In addition, they offered their workplaces or clients key skills unique to their community psychology training, particularly the interdisciplinary, multi-level, and collective approaches. Employers, colleagues, and clients appeared to appreciate the ideas and values espoused by community psychologists, leading to selection over other candidates, and a distinct profile in the workplace.

However, a majority of graduates saw their employers as rather unaware of these advantages. Indeed, graduates believed that employers were not seeking a 'community psychologist,' and could have appointed social scientists, health workers or graduates from a number of other backgrounds. Furthermore, some felt that their community psychology training had disappointed or failed them in their preparation for employment.

There is clearly a need in Aotearoa, New Zealand, for education of employers about the unique skills and approaches offered by those with community psychology training, as well as further work to improve the relevance of community psychology training.

# The Application
# of Community Psychology Principles
# in Diverse Settings

## John Kalafat

Rutgers University

**SUMMARY.** This paper describes the application of such community psychology principles of empowerment and systemic interventions in a variety of applied settings, including school systems, a university campus, and a community hospital. The consistent application of such principles illustrates one way in which a viable career as community psychologist can be maintained in settings that do not have community psychology positions per se. *[Article copies available for a fee from The Haworth Document Delivery Service: 1-800-342-9678. E-mail address: getinfo@haworthpressinc.com <Website: http://www.haworthpressinc.com>]*

**KEYWORDS.** Community psychology, consultation, program evaluation

Julian (1997) indicated that the practice of community psychology consists of the application of community psychology principles, the skills necessary to apply these principles, and settings in which these principles and skills can be applied. Those who are considering the

---

Address correspondence to: John Kalafat, Rutgers Graduate School of Applied and Professional Psychology, 152 Frelinghuysen Road, Piscataway, NJ 08854-8085.

This article is an expanded version of a column that appeared in *The Community Psychologist.*

[Haworth co-indexing entry note]: "The Application of Community Psychology Principles in Diverse Settings." Kalafat, John. Co-published simultaneously in *Journal of Prevention & Intervention in the Community* (The Haworth Press, Inc.) Vol. 19, No. 2, 2000, pp. 53-59; and: *Employment in Community Psychology: The Diversity of Opportunity* (ed: Clifford R. O'Donnell, and Joseph R. Ferrari) The Haworth Press, Inc., 2000, pp. 53-59. Single or multiple copies of this article are available for a fee from The Haworth Document Delivery Service [1-800-342-9678, 9:00 a.m. - 5:00 p.m. (EST). E-mail address: getinfo@haworthpressinc.com].

practice of community psychology as a career will find a good deal of consensus about community psychology principles, and a substantial body of skills that must be mastered. There is, however, a need for more explication of settings in which community psychologists can ply their trade. Ira Iscoe, an early leader in community psychology, put this succinctly when he asked, "Who will buy community psychology?"

Chavis (1993) and Weissberg (1995) suggested that the practice of community psychology is not well enough developed to provide a proven and secure employment option. This is probably true if one were to look for job listings in the applied sector that call for "community psychologists." However, the thesis of this paper is that a viable career as a community psychologist is possible through the application of community psychology principles in a wide variety of settings that do not appear as community psychology positions. Specific examples from the author's career as an Applied Community Psychologist will be used to illustrate these principles.

I became a community psychologist because my mentor (Bernie Bloom) suggested that such community psychology principles as prevention, empowerment, and systemic approaches would have a much greater impact than individually-based, waiting-mode approaches. Thus, while I received some training in traditional assessment and intervention skills, I chose graduate practica and internship experiences that afforded opportunities for community-oriented activities. These included consultation with Head Start centers and positions in a psychiatric emergency room, a comprehensive neighborhood service center (similar to today's family support programs), a youth-oriented free clinic, and a Consultation and Education (C & E) department of a Community Mental Health Center (CMHC). My first post-graduate position was at a university counseling center and I was asked to coordinate the campus outreach activities and co-found a campus hotline that we subsequently expanded to a regional crisis center. These graduate and initial post-graduate positions helped me to develop consultation, community organization, and administrative experiences that opened subsequent career doors.

In each of the applied positions that I have held, no one was buying community psychology per se, but they *were* interested in buying community-related skills such as program planning and evaluation, organizational development, consultation, and training. Those interested in the practice of community psychology must also develop expertise in marketable content areas such as crisis intervention, social problem solving, substance abuse prevention, and the like. Such skills and content areas helped me to obtain a number of positions and, once credibility in the settings was established, there were increasing opportunities to apply community psychology principles. Following are examples of the application of these principles in diverse settings, including a university campus, secondary school systems, and a medical center corporation. Additional examples could be provided were it not for space limitations.

## UNIVERSITY COUNSELING CENTER

The position of UCC Director provided the opportunity to complement the traditional "waiting-mode" services with campus-wide initiatives that addressed the broad university mission of student support and retention and involved the application of community psychology principles of prevention, empowerment, community building, collaboration, and ecological or systemic interventions.

Research had shown that most students who dropped out did so in their first year, and that many cited the lack of a sense of community as a contributing factor. Undergraduate and graduate students were trained to lead first-year student orientation groups that were expanded to year-long support and resource groups. These students formed the core of a number of initiatives that resulted in the counseling center becoming the central clearinghouse for the selection and training of resident assistants, tutors, Upward Bound, and Economic Opportunity counselors; and, eventually, training for faculty advisors and campus security personnel. Through these training programs, the counseling center established relationships with other campus support services. We were able to take the lead in the development of a coordinated campus emergency response procedure, and a campus interagency council that fostered greater communication and coordination among campus services. These programs not only empowered and increased the sense of community among students and campus service providers, but also enhanced the overall supportive climate of the campus.

Currently, such service integration initiatives are occurring in communities throughout the country, many of which are funded through the Child and Adolescent Service System Program (CASSP) of the National Institute of Mental Health (Illback & Neill, 1995). Thus, there are opportunities for community psychologists to become involved in such activities in both campus and community settings.

## *SCHOOL SYSTEMS*

Subsequent positions as director of a Consultation and Education (C & E) department of a CMHC, and consultant in a free-standing community consultation and evaluation organization provided access to secondary school systems. In the C & E position, I collaborated with school personnel to develop and evaluate a school-based youth suicide prevention program. This ecological program aimed to enhance the ability of adults, students, and school-community systems to identify, respond to, and obtain help for at-risk youth. It included training for administrators, faculty, parents, community gatekeepers, and students; the establishment of crisis response teams and procedures; and, the promotion of linkages between schools and community agencies. Recent research indicates that involvement with the school and contact with caring adults are significant protective factors that moderate a number of risk behaviors (McBride et al., 1995). This has led to current efforts to combine domain-specific prevention programs with school-based social bonding programs that employ empowerment, ecological, and community building principles.

The consultation and evaluation organization held a number of state contracts and grants, one of which was to evaluate Kentucky's statewide school-based family resource/youth services center program. This program is a leading example of the growing national family support (Kagan & Weissbourd, 1994) and school-based services (Dryfoos, 1994) movements. These programs seek to increase the involvement of students and families in schools and to forge linkages among schools, communities, and families to address barriers to student learning and development. They involve the application of empowerment, prevention, ecological, community building, and collaboration principles. Our implementation evaluation of these centers provided an opportunity to document their application of such principles. As part of an action research approach, we drew on our findings to collaborate with program personnel in the development of a center coordinator training and mentoring program.

We found that these school-based centers were exemplars of community psychology principles, and, as with school-based prevention and wellness promotion programs, provide many opportunities for the practice of community psychology.

## ORGANIZATIONAL SETTING

Following the C & E position, I assumed the position of Director of Education for the medical corporation that sponsored the CMHC. In this position, my staff and I worked with the CEO and vice presidents to implement a Total Quality Management (TQM) program. TQM is grounded in the systems and organizational principles of Deming (1986) that have considerable overlap with community psychology principles.

TQM emphasizes that all departments, vendors, and customers are one interdependent system. That system is made up of many work processes that are best improved and maintained by teams of empowered employees. The organizational structure becomes an inverted pyramid in which the CEO empowers managers, who empower workers, who serve the customers, who define service quality. The focus is on data based preventive efforts rather than attempts to address problems as they arise on a case by case basis. Over a five year period, teams of managers and employees instituted a number of changes in work processes that resulted in significant savings and the achievement of the goal of becoming ranked in the top 5% of medical centers rated by the Joint Commission of the Accreditation of Healthcare Organizations.

In each of these positions, my interventions were consistently informed by community psychology principles. These interventions initially addressed felt needs of the organizations through the provision of direct services, and subsequently evolved into preventive, empowering, collaborative, and systemic interventions.

It must be noted that often these principles are not easy to sell. For example, person-centered, deficit-oriented approaches are deeply entrenched in most settings. There is substantial pressure in mental health services, counseling centers, and school-based services to maintain large individual caseloads. For a variety of reasons, including a history of competing for resources, there is resistance to collaboration among departments within organizations, and among different agencies (White & Wehlage, 1995). In most applied settings, there is little time or resources for research and evaluation, unless these are included in contracts and grants. Finally, it is very difficult for managers or school officials to give up control and empower employees and students. It is important to be able to articulate the practical benefits of the application of these principles, as well as to address the concerns that are often raised in regard to them. It is also important to collect qualitative and quantitative data that document their impact.

## CLOSING NOTE TO NEW PROFESSIONALS

It is likely that those community psychology principles that are emphasized in one's practice are a function of one's mentors, the context of one's practice, and one's personal inclinations. There are two interrelated principles that have consistently informed my practice over the years. The first is an emphasis on ecological interventions, or those that seek to change systems more than individuals. The second, empowerment flows from the first because in order to effect change in a system it is necessary to have the active involvement of all of the stakeholders in that system. Thus, in some of the examples from this paper, we promoted the participation of all workers, managers, and executives in efforts to develop more efficient work process. Or, we promoted student and campus gatekeeper involvement in the development of more a supportive and responsive environment that helped students through the transition to college. In my experience, these approaches have yielded more pervasive and robust changes than individual, deficit-based approaches, and have permitted me to function as a community psychologist in each position that I have held.

## REFERENCES

Chavis, D. (1993). A future for community psychology practice. *American Journal of Community Psychology, 21*, 171-183.

Deming, W. E. (1986). *Out of crisis.* Cambridge, Mass: MIT, Center for Advanced Engineering Study.

Dryfoos, J. G. (1994). *Full-service schools.* San Francisco: Jossey-Bass.

Illback, R. J., & Neill, T. K. (1995). Service coordination in mental health systems for children, youth, and families: Progress, problems, prospects. *Journal of Mental Health Administration, 22*, 17-28.

Julian, D. (1997). Advancing the goals of the Society for Community Research and Action: A definition of community psychology. *The Community Psychologist, 30,* 26-27.

Kagan, S. L., & Weissbourd, B. (1994). *Putting families first.* San Francisco: Jossey-Bass.

Weissberg, R. (1995). Reflections on training and job market issues as community psychology enters its fourth decade. *The Community Psychologist, 28,* 3-5.

White, J. A., & Wehlage, G. (1995). Community collaboration: If it is such a good idea, why is it so hard to do? *Educational Evaluation and Policy Analysis, 17,* 23-28.

# Community Research and Action
# in a Local United Way Organization

## David A. Julian

The United Way

**SUMMARY.** This paper provides a brief description of the planning and evaluation function at the United Way in Franklin County, OH. Examples of principles of community research and action and community psychology that are incorporated in aspects of this function are highlighted. Organizations like United Ways are ideal settings in the local community in which to practice community research and action. Implementation of outcomes-based funding is used as an example of how a community psychologist might influence local policies and practices in the human services arena. A number of suggestions for students interested in applied careers are offered. *[Article copies available for a fee from The Haworth Document Delivery Service: 1-800-342-9678. E-mail address: getinfo@haworthpressinc.com <Website: http://www.haworthpressinc.com>]*

**KEYWORDS.** Community psychology, United Way, program evaluation, public policy

I am currently employed by the United Way in Columbus/Franklin County, Ohio. Franklin County is a major urban center with a metropolitan population exceeding one million individuals. The applied

---

Address correspondence to: David A. Julian, United Way of Franklin County, 360 South Third Street, Columbus, OH 43215-5485.

[Haworth co-indexing entry note]: "Community Research and Action in a Local United Way Organization." Julian, David A. Co-published simultaneously in *Journal of Prevention & Intervention in the Community* (The Haworth Press, Inc.) Vol. 19, No. 2, 2000, pp. 61-65; and: *Employment in Community Psychology: The Diversity of Opportunity* (ed: Clifford R. O'Donnell, and Joseph R. Ferrari) The Haworth Press, Inc., 2000, pp. 61-65. Single or multiple copies of this article are available for a fee from The Haworth Document Delivery Service [1-800-342-9678, 9:00 a.m. - 5:00 p.m. (EST). E-mail address: getinfo@haworthpressinc.com].

work in which I am engaged directly involves community research and action, and I believe my training as a community psychologist enhances my ability to function successfully at United Way. The point in writing this essay is to encourage current and prospective graduate students in community psychology and other social action-oriented disciplines to consider applied careers and to look to non-traditional employers like United Ways for jobs.

After graduate school, I was interested in working in a setting where I could be involved in planning and evaluation of local human services programs. My prior training and work experience included a Master of City and Regional Planning degree and five years tenure as the "Director of Information Services" at a local human services planning agency. As Director of Information Services, I was responsible for compiling and disseminating local human services needs assessment and evaluation data. United Way was a primary consumer of this information. My experiences as a human services planner made United Way a natural choice when it was time to find a job that encompassed community research and action.

## COMMUNITY RESEARCH AND ACTION

Julian (1997) defines applied community psychology as the application of the principles of community psychology to solve social problems. Some principles of community psychology focus on prevention, collaboration, evaluation, empowerment, citizen participation and social policy (Orford, 1992). Many system-level planning and evaluation positions in organizations like local United Ways are likely to offer opportunities to apply the principles of community psychology on a regular and consistent basis.

## UNITED WAY AS A SETTING
## FOR COMMUNITY RESEARCH AND ACTION

There are more than 1,000 local United Ways in the U.S. (United Way of America, 1996). It is likely that local United Ways will raise and invest more than three billion dollars in health and human services at the local level in 1998 (American Association of Fund Raising

Counsel, 1992). United Ways offer unique opportunities to practice community research and action. In many communities, United Ways are leaders in efforts to address local human services issues. United Ways typically convene and support citizen committees that define community priorities and distribute financial resources to local health and human services organizations. United Way staff provide technical support and empower such committees to effect local policies. The technical support role provides the opportunity to impact local issues in a significant way and to bring community research and action to the local community.

In my tenure, the planning and evaluation function at United Way encompassed a variety of roles. I have been identified as an evaluator, planner, facilitator, researcher, trainer and change agent. For example, as a United Way staff member, I have participated in the evaluation of specific initiatives designed to improve local services delivery; provided staff support and leadership to a community level planning committee that defined local human services needs; facilitated the development of community objectives that guided investment decisions; researched methods for measuring community progress in achieving specific human services goals; trained and provided technical assistance related to outcomes-based funding to more than 60 health and human services organizations; and contributed to a major system change effort to implement outcomes-based funding.

## OUTCOMES-BASED FUNDING

The effort to implement outcomes-based funding within the United Way system may serve as an example of how a community research and action agenda can influence local policy. Outcomes-based funding places great emphasis on defining and measuring results at the program and community levels and investing resources accordingly (United Way of America, 1995). Staff and community volunteers are positioning United Ways throughout the country as leaders in the outcomes-based funding movement (Bell, 1997; United Way of America, 1996).

In the last three years, designing and implementing outcomes-based funding has been a high priority for the United Way in Franklin County. The structure of the model developed by the United Way was based on adaptations of models used in several communities and the work of prominent evaluation theorists (Patton, 1997). United Way planners and community volunteers adapted outcomes-based funding methods for implementation in the local community; gained consensus that such an effort would result in improved services and greater accountability; and initiated the implementation of new organizational practices.

The Franklin County effort to implement outcomes-based funding is based on the definition of "critical need areas" and related community objectives. The six critical need areas include: (1) education; (2) employment; (3) health; (4) housing; (5) race relations; and (6) safety. The primary structures for addressing the six critical need areas are community action committees referred to as Vision Councils. There are currently six Vision Councils corresponding to critical need areas. Vision Councils are composed of 35 to 40 community members representing various constituencies such as human services agencies, congregations, businesses, educational institutions and government.

Vision Council members have defined specific community objectives related to each critical need area and are currently engaged in the process of defining relevant problem solving strategies. Objectives and strategies provide a means of focusing United Way and other community effort on critical issues. For example, Health Vision Council members defined reducing teen smoking from 31 to 25 percent over the next three to five years as a community objective. Tools available to Vision Council members include public policy initiatives; collaborations with other community partners; health promotion and other media strategies; and investment in traditional human services programs.

## RECOMMENDATIONS TO STUDENTS

The planning and evaluation function at United Way experience suggests several recommendations to students interested in community research and action-oriented careers:

1. Seek a community placement with a prospective employer and consider conducting your dissertation research in this setting.
2. Select a dissertation topic focused on an issue of interest to the prospective employer and produce a product that has the potential to influence policy.
3. Work for an organization that controls the allocation of significant community resources. Such organizations typically have great influence over the local community's agenda and operating procedures.

4. Develop marketable skills in areas such as consensus building, program evaluation and communications.
5. Take course work outside of your major discipline. Urban planning, social work and business may offer opportunities to develop skills that will prove particularly valuable in applied settings.
6. Think of contributors and donors (people who provide financial support for human services programs) as customers, explicitly define the product you produce and demonstrate the value of that product.

The intention in describing the planning and evaluation function at United Way was to provide some insight into what has been an interesting and fulfilling career path. Local United Ways and other human services delivery systems may be ideal settings in which to practice community research and action. Community psychologists and other community research and action-oriented professionals may be uniquely positioned to influence planning and evaluation practices in such organizations. In my experience, United Way has provided considerable opportunity to be involved in significant local, health and human services issues in a manner consistent with the principles of community research and action.

## REFERENCES

American Association of Fund Raising Counsel. (1992). *Giving USA.* (Available from AAFRC Trust for Philanthropy, 25 West 43rd Street, New York, NY 10036.)

Bell, J. (1997, December). *A unique undertaking: The National Learning Project on using program outcome data to create measurable change.* Presentation at the United Way of America, Advanced Issues in Focusing on Program Outcomes Meeting, Washington D.C.

Julian, D. A. (1997). Advancing the goals of the Society for Community Research and Action: A definition of applied community psychology. *The Community Psychologist, 30,* 26-27.

Orford, J. (1992). *Community psychology: Theory and practice.* New York: John Wiley and Sons.

Patton, M. Q. (1997). *Utilization focused evaluation.* Thousand Oaks, CA: Sage.

United Way of America. (1996). *1996 Membership directory.* (Available from United Way of America, 701 North Fairfax Street, Alexandria, VA 22314-2045.)

United Way of America. (1995). *Measuring program outcomes: A practical approach.* (Available from United Way of America, 701 N. Fairfax St., Alexandria, VA 22314-2045).

# Program Evaluation and Prevention in Child Welfare

## Benjamin Kerman

Casey Family Services

**SUMMARY.** Individuals with interests in children and families, as well as in critically examining interventions and service systems may consider opportunities for evaluation research in Child Welfare. As the field increasingly adopts multi-level preventative interventions, positions may offer opportunities for motivated individuals with skills in articulating and examining phenomena at individual, family, community and organizational levels. The paper follows one pathway from graduate school to a position within an organizational context manifesting many of the major themes in contemporary community psychology, including capacity building and empowerment, community development and multi-level prevention interventions, consumer involvement and the stimulating role of program evaluation. The purposeful collection of practical experience is suggested as an important balance to rigorous academic preparation and creative exploration of different professional roles. *[Article copies available for a fee from The Haworth Document Delivery Service: 1-800-342-9678. E-mail address: getinfo@haworthpressinc.com <Website: http://www.haworthpressinc.com>]*

**KEYWORDS.** Community psychology, child welfare, prevention, program evaluation

---

Address correspondence to: Benjamin Kerman, Casey Family Services, One Corporate Drive, Suite 515, Shelton, CT 06484.

The author thanks the Family Advocacy and Support Team in Casey Family Services' Vermont Division, as well as his colleagues in the Research Department.

[Haworth co-indexing entry note]: "Program Evaluation and Prevention in Child Welfare." Kerman, Benjamin. Co-published simultaneously in *Journal of Prevention & Intervention in the Community* (The Haworth Press, Inc.) Vol. 19, No. 2, 2000, pp. 67-73; and: *Employment in Community Psychology: The Diversity of Opportunity* (ed: Clifford R. O'Donnell, and Joseph R. Ferrari) The Haworth Press, Inc., 2000, pp. 67-73. Single or multiple copies of this article are available for a fee from The Haworth Document Delivery Service [1-800-342-9678, 9:00 a.m. - 5:00 p.m. (EST). E-mail address: getinfo@haworthpress inc.com].

Six months ago, I began collaborating with direct care child and family clinicians in a private foundation-affiliated child welfare agency. My full-time position as Research Associate at Casey Family Services (CT) represents a nexus for my personal development as scientist-practitioner, my preparation in Clinical and Community Psychology and my action research orientation. After briefly highlighting the genesis of some of my values, I will describe one example of a current effort to address community level targets for prevention in Child Welfare settings. This emerging program reflects the evolution of the traditional Family Support Service approach. The program embodies several major trends in Community Psychology, including polymorphous empowerment, Community Development and multi-level intervention, consumer involvement and the stimulating role of program evaluation.

*Formative Career Development*: The *APA Monitor* advertisement for this position ignited my interest, appealing to my long-held interests in community-based program evaluation, multi-disciplinary collaboration and child-oriented family interventions. Idiosyncratic intrapsychic and internecine early influences aside, my interest in working with youth and families dates back at least to my undergraduate Psychology training. My desire for a respite from my studies, practical exposure to mental health and my reading of Goffman's classic *Asylums* (1961) led me to seek a position as mental health worker with children and adolescents in a nearby psychiatric hospital. Although sustained by contacts with several inspiring individual staff members, I was troubled by the challenges to treatment coordination, inadequate training and support for the omnipresent line staff, the wide gap between expected outcomes and resources dedicated to milieu treatment, and the obstacles to constructive self-reflection. I charted my course for Clinical Psychology graduate school to earn my credentials and become a reform-minded child and family program developer.

Galvanized by an advisor's critique of my potential application, I first sought more clinical and research experience. Breaking free from the total institutions of asylum and undergraduate college, I worked as a community-based outreach counselor with court-involved teens and their families. I enjoyed a panoramic perspective of integrated services, working at the crossroads of a diverse network of services (e.g., courts, community services, state agencies, the schools, etc.) and activities (i.e., individual treatment, parent training, support groups, case management). After one more year as a hospital-based research assistant working with adults with chronic mental illness, I felt ready to return to school.

In considering graduate programs, I was attracted to the University of Rhode Island because my interests corresponded closely with the strengths of the program. Although my coursework was oriented toward the Clinical subdiscipline, a number of additional classes in substantive (e.g., Primary Prevention, Consultation and Community-based Health Promotion) and methodological areas (e.g., Program Evaluation, several statistics courses) proved invaluable ingredients in my preparation. Academic classes provided the foundation for a diverse exposure to settings and roles, including individual psychotherapy practice with adults, membership in a family systems therapy team, and two years of part-time work at a community mental health center in an economically impoverished city.

A key learning opportunity came with my affiliation with the Community Research and Services Team. Working as a graduate assistant evaluating several community-based prevention partnership grants, we provided process and outcome feedback to a network of AODA prevention task forces and their umbrella coalition. I learned through observation and practice, applying newly-acquired research skills to examine citizen participation, consultation and technical assistance and community development models applied to prevention and health promotion. With the support of my major professor, I pursued my interests in multi-level research. The naturalistic setting allowed research impossible in the lab or campus settings, such as identifying factors associated with individual empowerment, collective empowerment and organizational features of empowering collectives (e.g., MacMillan, Florin, Stevenson, Kerman & Mitchell, 1995).

I completed my required internship and an additional clinical postdoc at the Yale Child Study Center. I was drawn there equally by the depth of assessment and therapy training and the espousal of a multi-level developmental framework for understanding, intervening and setting social policy to benefit children and families. Among many lasting impacts, my involvement with the Child Development-Community Policing program (CDCP) was pivotal in helping me appreciate the integration of clinical work with other contextual influences, multi-disciplinary collaboration, organizational change and prevention. In this partnership, mental health professionals and police exchange expertise in a language available to each partner: Fellowship seminars for the police foster officers' understanding of child development and the child, family and community's response to trauma concretized within the community policing setting. Similarly, clinical seminars, crime scene consultations and joint case conferences create opportunities for involvement in the broader context of the clients presenting problems, as well as earlier intervention for clients who demonstrate staggeringly high morbidity and treatment attrition rates (Marans, 1994). In addition to the secondary preventive functions, the project promotes individual and organizational relationships that aim to prevent legal and health problems, supporting the growth of less adversarial problem-solving relationships between police and neighborhoods.

*Child Welfare*: The field of Child Welfare represents a vibrant interdisciplinary landscape for integrating emerging preventive and therapeutic interventions. Agencies historically concerned with caring for the child "victims" of incompetent parents, providing alternative settings for affected children (e.g., foster family care), are increasingly involved with multiple level preventive interventions. Energized by a growing awareness of the community-level roots of a range of social problems impacting children and families, agencies are nurturing programs which redefine child- or family-focused programs to encompass community-level action.

Prototypic Family Support programs aim to strengthen parents in their roles as nurturing caregivers and providers (Weissbourd & Kagan, 1989). At Casey, one team is exploring the impact of expanding the traditional direct and indirect services for individuals and families associated with the generic model to include advocacy and community development work (e.g., time limited counseling, psychoeducation) while abandoning the traditionally disempowering professional-client relationship. Using a post-modern narrative family-centered approach, families articulate their needs, set their goals, determine treatment teams, evaluate their progress, etc. The team extends the impact advocating for a more inclusive process in multiple community sectors. For example, team members actively advocate for the inclusion of consumers in traditionally professionals-only collectives, while at the same time supporting initiatives to increase partnership efficacy and the amount of resources available for specific prevention programming. The community level goals include building the capacity of the service community to spark programming more responsive to community needs. For example, the staff are making presentations at other agencies and negotiating with several other providers to build a coalition of agencies with shared interests to decrease the counterproductive costs associated with duplication and unnecessary competition. These interagency network-strengthening activities can thereby make services more accessible and affordable, while strengthening the institutional fabric of a community.

A major thrust in my current activities involves supporting self-examination among innovative program teams. The research department at Casey Family Services functions as an internal support system, facilitating reflective practice and building the agency's capacity for self-evaluation (Federman, 1996). As the direct operating arm of the Annie E. Casey Foundation, CFS seeks to develop, improve, document and disseminate successful, cost-effective child-centered family-focused services across the spectrum of needs, including long term foster care, intensive treatment foster care, family reunification, family preservation and post-adoption interventions. In addition to consultation regarding "best practices" and pursuit of a number of pragmatic applied research projects (e.g., a follow-up of adults formerly in foster care), we help the teams articulate their models of change, specify evaluation plans, collect data, interpret the results and disseminate the findings.

In addition to the obvious connections to my academic preparation in measurement, as well as individual, family, neighborhood and organizational change processes, the work also draws heavily on consultation skills. Through a series of meetings with social workers, family support workers, team leaders and perhaps consumers, consensus descriptions of conditions targeted, goals set and program components are hammered out. This leads to the formulation and operationalizing of expected output and consequent outcomes, as well as the development of an evaluation plan and the team's collection of data for self-evaluation and program improvement. This facilitated process is exciting and challenging as is any research-practice collaboration: The program evaluator often needs to translate the languages of board members and frontline practitioners, intuitive clinicians and empirical scientists, seeking to co-discover a balance between the competing demands. This way, my current position continues to help me build consultation skills founded conceptually in the classroom and seasoned initially in a community-based externship and research assistantships.

Paralleling developments in other areas of human services, child welfare organizations have increasingly taken a multi-level approach to include community empowerment and development of local institutions to manage planned change. Reconceptualizing and redesigning child welfare services to benefit families beyond the caseload presents an exciting challenge. While the trend toward context complexity and interventions at higher levels of social structure is being fostered by the public sector (e.g., OSAP Partnerships), foundations (AECF Community Initiatives grants) and individual agencies (see Feikema, Segalavich & Jeffries, 1997), agencies new to thinking at the community level are faced with needs for new theoretical models and change technology. Clearly, there is a dramatic opportunity for evaluation collaborators who can observe and articulate processes and outcomes at multiple levels.

*The Advice*: In reflecting on my journey so far, I realize that 'two paths diverged in a wood,' and my program evaluation work has permitted me to follow both. While I hope Frost excuses my paraphrase, I think that one of the keys to my being happy has been a commitment to pursue my passions and curiosity melding Community and Clinical interests. For me, diverse experiential learning has been helpful to the extent it has been purposeful: While trying different roles and settings, it has been central for me to develop my own family, preserving the compass headings at home and work. Seize the precious opportunity to creatively muse on the ideal (e.g., graduate program, internship or job) and then go look for it. Don't be too discouraged if it takes a series of successive approximations. Career development, like good service planning, requires not only forethought, but collaboration, shaping and improvisation.

## REFERENCES

Federman, D. M. (1996). Empowerment evaluation: Introduction to theory and practice. In Federman, D. M., Kaftarian, S. J., & Wandersman, A. (Eds.). *Empowerment Evaluation: Knowledge and Tools for Self Assessment & Accountability.* Thousand Oaks, CA: Sage Publications, 3-48.

Goffman, E. (1961). *Asylums: Essays on the social situation of mental patients and other inmates.* New York: Anchor Doubleday.

Feikema, R. J., Segalavich, J. H. & Jeffries, S. H. (1997). From child development to community development: One agency's journey. *Families in Society: The Journal of Contemporary Human Services, 77,* 185-195.

Marans, S. (1994). Community violence and children's development: Collaborative Interventions. In Chiland, C. & Young, J. G. (Eds.), *The child in the family: Volume 11. Children and Violence* (pp. 109-124). London: Jason Aronson.

McMillan, B., Florin, P., Stevenson, J., Kerman, B. & Mitchell, R. E. (1995). Empowerment praxis in community coalitions. *American Journal of Community Psychology, 23*(5), 699-726.

Weissbourd, B. & Kagan, S. L., (1989). Family support programs: Catalysts for change. *American Journal of Orthopsychiatry, 59*(1), 20-31.

# Making Dreams Come True

Deanna Parker Knapp

University of Kansas School of Medicine-Wichita

**SUMMARY.** A master's degree in community psychology can open doors, allow for vast opportunities, and be a catalyst to help dreams come true. As this article points out, it also can help unite over 140 agencies in seeking collaborative funding and networking or help to decrease gang violence. Community psychology is the degree for the future. As advocates, facilitators, policy analysts and mediators, community psychologists can handle change, assess situations, environments, and resources, seek alternate solutions, and problem-solve. These individuals are able to focus on client expectations, listen to differing opinions, and then seek common ground, resolve conflict, and elicit feedback. There is not a company or agency that will not appreciate these talents in the next millennium. *[Article copies available for a fee from The Haworth Document Delivery Service: 1-800-342-9678. E-mail address: getinfo@haworthpressinc.com <Website: http://www.haworthpressinc.com>]*

**KEYWORDS.** Community psychology, empowerment

One never realizes the avenues that will be available to them with a community psychology degree. For this Wichita State University (WSU) graduate, the first path led to the Department of Family of the University of Kansas School of Medicine-Wichita and Community

---

Address correspondence to: Deanna Parker Knapp, MA, Director of Research, University of Kansas School of Medicine-Wichita, 1010 North Kansas, Suite 3054, Wichita, KS 67214-3199 (e-mail: dknapp@kumc.edu).

[Haworth co-indexing entry note]: "Making Dreams Come True." Knapp, Deanna Parker. Co-published simultaneously in *Journal of Prevention & Intervention in the Community* (The Haworth Press, Inc.) Vol. 19, No. 2, 2000, pp. 75-81; and: *Employment in Community Psychology: The Diversity of Opportunity* (ed: Clifford R. O'Donnell, and Joseph R. Ferrari) The Haworth Press, Inc., 2000, pp. 75-81. Single or multiple copies of this article are available for a fee from The Haworth Document Delivery Service [1-800-342-9678, 9:00 a.m. - 5:00 p.m. (EST). E-mail address: getinfo@haworthpressinc.com].

75

Medicine. I was hired as a research associate in the Research and Development Unit (REDU). My main task was to assist family medicine faculty with any aspect of their research projects. The director of REDU told me that he had every intention of hiring another person until he met her. When he saw the skills that community psychology had given me, he made the job offer before they ended their first interview.

The transition from community psychology to family and community medicine was a relatively easy one for me. The basic philosophies of both areas are very similar. Both believe in looking at the whole person, not just one aspect of an individual. They study the impact of the family, social networking, community, and individual behaviors on the well-being of the person. Both strive to provide the individual with whatever resources the person needs to live a fulfilling life. Community psychology and family and community medicine empower their patients/clients by encouraging them to make decisions about their well-being. As advocates for serving the whole person, these programs emphasize prevention and early intervention. Community psychology and family and community medicine programs work to change health attitudes, incorporate healthy changes in behavior, and focus on wellness.

Shortly after joining family medicine, I approached the chairperson of the department and the director of REDU about pursuing my interest in working with not-for-profit agencies. This interest evolved not only from my community psychology studies and practicum experiences, but also from the course work in the *Certificate of Non-profit Management* program. While working on my master's, I obtained this certificate from WSU's Center for Management Development. The certificate program covered such topics as working with boards of directors, fundraising, preparing volunteer boards and financial management of not-for-profits.

The Family and Community Medicine chairperson and director of REDU agreed that by assisting not-for-profit agencies, the department was able to serve a larger community. As part of this outreach, I applied for and received my first grant to do a community needs assessment of the services being provided to children from birth through three years of age. The needs assessment helped to create a coalition of service providers and assist them in consolidating services. The survey also showed some serious shortcomings, such as the fact that only one percent of the agencies were seeking grant-funding.

My graduate course work and practicum experiences in needs assessments and third party evaluations enabled me to assist many not-for-profit agencies. The revenue from the contracted services helped to solidify the chairperson's decision to continue allowing me to work in the community and do the duties of a research associate.

The next two years were superb. REDU's contracts were doing great. Family medicine faculty and residents were pursuing multiple research endeavors. The department had several grants that were keeping REDU busy, and I was nine months pregnant with my first child. I was content and was not seeking a change. So, of course, I was approached about leaving family medicine and providing these same services for the whole campus. I had my mind set that a new baby was enough change for me to handle. Needless to say, the Associate Dean for Research can be very persuasive. The day before my son was born, I began overseeing the operations of the university's Office of Research.

I had my hands a little more than full and if it were not for the traits of tenacity and empowerment taught in community psychology, I may have felt overwhelmed. As is often the case of a university's research administration office, the division had a prior reputation for being a hindrance to faculty and their research. The Associate Dean for Research wanted this reputation reversed. I and the office were to do whatever it took to encourage research and provide their researchers with the resources they needed. He told me that he did not like the word "no," and neither did the other faculty. The office was to find a way to serve its customers and get "yes" answers to their requests.

The first task was to change the mindset of the research staff. In order to provide excellent comprehensive services, the office had to move from the policing mentality to a resource team approach. No matter which research staff member a faculty person approached, that person had to be able to provide excellent services. Too many things were delayed in the research office because no one was willing to make a decision. Empowering people who were not used to making decisions and who had been discouraged to take risks required tenacity.

My Graduate Research Assistantship (GRA) enabled me to handle the management issue in the Office of Research. As a GRA, I managed Wichita State University's Social Science Research Lab. In the lab, I oversaw the staff, budgets, workloads, and customer service. So, I had an idea of the complexities of an office and the tenacity required in running a shop.

Today, the Office of Research is not only known for being a resource for its campus, it also assists faculty on its sister campus and several agencies in the community. Its motto is "Your Resource for Research." The research team has gone out of its way to live up to the motto.

To determine the future direction of the research office, the research team annually conducts needs assessments, focus groups, and/or faculty interviews. Several new programs and services have been developed from the responses. The office now offers services that are not considered standard for a research administration office, but the faculty and staff made it clear that these were the aids that would best assist them. In the upcoming year, the research team hopes to take its customer services to yet another level by providing in-house research associates, a biostatistican and a faculty grant-writing mentor. The planning committee for this upgrade includes a sampling of clients, administration, and the research team. By including these key players, it knows that the upgrade will be in line with our clients' needs. It also knows that the research team can feasibly do it. Shared decision-making is another community psychology philosophy that has served me well.

I often tell people that I have the best job in the world. I get to help make dreams come true. Faculty and staff come to me and my team with a dream or an idea. They find the funding and help pull together the proposal. With a little luck, and a lot of tenacity, those dreams often become realities.

For example, a couple of years ago, Mae Ellen Terrebonne, M.D., a pediatrician, came to me because I was upset about the number of children wounded by gang violence. She was tired of seeing "babies" in the Emergency Room.

Together they developed a grant proposal for the Department of Justice. The proposal put a prevention program in the community that brought together gang members, parents, community leaders, police officers, teachers and youth nine years of age and younger.

Dr. Terrebonne got her wish and the response from the community was great. All of the groups became involved, especially the gang members. They were very enthusiastic about the idea because they did not want to see their younger siblings become involved in gangs.

The Associate Dean for Research has encouraged continued services to not-for-profit agencies. In my first year with the Office of Research, I wrote a grant proposal to the Howard Hughes Medical Institute to enhance the biomedical education for minority students. The concept was to bring together a medical school, an independent research institute, a community organization and the school district to encourage minorities to choose biomedical careers. They were awarded a five-year grant and I was asked to the speak to the Howard Hughes Medical Institute about "this unique idea of collaborating such services." This concept is not unique to community psychology. Don't community psychologists already pull together the best possible players to provide the most effective services? Community psychologists know the importance of collaboration and involving key resources.

In line with the collaborative emphasis of community psychology, Robert Hull, Information Specialist for WSU's Office of Research, and I co-founded the Kansas Professional Grant Association (KPGA). From my earlier assessment of agencies serving children birth to three, I knew that these agencies were seeking just a handful of grants and missing some great opportunities.

The *Psychological Service Agencies* class taught by Fr. Ken Yates, my practicums, the *Certificate of Non-profit Management* program and my previous contractual work offered great insight to the challenges these not-for-profits faced. Fr. Yates advised the students that good-hearted people run some of the not-for-profit agencies with few management skills. Thus, these people can find themselves in some difficult situations and short on revenue. Keeping in mind Fr. Yates' lessons on "good-hearted" administrators, Robert Hull and I felt there may be a real need for a network of not-for-profit grant writers or those who wanted to write for grants.

Robert and I hoped that at least 20 people would have an interest in such a network. They sent out 50 invitations. At the first session, 52 attended and five others called and requested to be on the mailing list. A year and a half later, to our great surprise, we had 140 members. The membership consists mainly of not-for-profit agencies, but several local grant-making foundations also liked the idea.

Robert and I realized that their universities had access to grant-funding resources that the not-for-profits could not afford. With this knowledge in hand, we set up resource centers in our respective offices. KPGA members are welcome to use the resource centers and search for funding opportunities. The centers also contain books, software, and workbooks on writing grants, working with boards and volunteers. As Dr. Greg Meissen, WSU professor, said in the *Community Psychology Course,* "Information is power–so give it away."

To determine the agendas for the KPGA meetings, Robert and I surveyed the members of KPGA. The members stated that networking and training were their top priorities, so at their quarterly meetings, we try to provide some training as well as time for people to interact. Each meeting is held at a different agency so KPGA does not become identified with only one agency or one person.

Another goal of the group is to encourage collaboration between not-for-profit agencies in seeking funding and in sharing resources. A few agencies have collaborated on applications and the KPGA foundation members have highly encouraged the not-for-profit agencies to do so.

For the first year, Robert and I coordinated all aspects of KPGA. Recently, we developed subcommittees to run different aspects of the association. Thus, the members are taking ownership of KPGA. Subcommittees oversee membership, publications, programs, workshops, and a steering committee. Robert and I continue to be involved but not in the forefront. For KPGA to really work, the agencies have to make it their own and determine the direction.

Several of the directors or development officers of these KPGA agencies are graduates from WSU's Community Psychology program. The meetings often feel like homecoming week and often resemble the discussions they had in some of the graduate classes. At the time, preparation for those graduate classes seemed excessive, since they were expected to come to the session "as if you are going into a test."

Reality is that this requirement made for some dynamic interactions. The community psychologist class consisted mostly of non-traditional students with the average age in the mid-thirties and already working in human services. Their work experiences added validity to the concepts being taught. They were able to take theories and applications from the texts and relate them to daily events. In KPGA, the students from this graduate program continue to network.

If any of them need information, a connection, or a resource, it is only a telephone call away.

In my opinion, community psychology is the degree of the future. It prepares one to handle change, assess situations, environments, and resources, seek alternate solutions, and problem-solve. Graduates are trained to be advocates, facilitators, policy analysts, and mediators. The course work and practicums prepare one to deal with client expectations, listen to differing opinions and then seek common ground, resolve conflict, and elicit feedback. There is a renewed, conscientious move to govern resource allocation and to make sure all programs are truly effective. In the next millennium, all professions are going to need professionals that have the skills, backgrounds, and education that the community psychology programs provide. Perhaps several of you will someday be making dreams come true.

# What a Long, Strange Trip It's Been: The Career Path of a Policy-Oriented Community Psychologist

Brian L. Wilcox

University of Nebraska

**SUMMARY.** Career paths are often shaped by chance factors. The author describes some of those factors that led him first to the field of psychology, then to the field of community psychology, and finally to a career bridging community psychology and public policy. Although chance factors influenced the author's career path, the author describes those elements of his graduate and postgraduate experience which prepared him to become a non-traditional policy-oriented community psychologist, as well as some of the characteristics needed to work effectively in policy settings. *[Article copies available for a fee from The Haworth Document Delivery Service: 1-800-342-9678. E-mail address: getinfo@haworthpressinc.com <Website: http://www.haworthpressinc.com>]*

**KEYWORDS.** Community psychology, public policy

While there is an extensive body of theory and research addressing the factors that shape career development and choice, the "theory" that seems to best account for the twisting path my career has taken

Address correspondence to: Brian L. Wilcox, Center on Children, Families, and the Law, 121 South 13th Street, Suite 302, Lincoln, NE 68588-0227 (email: bwilcox @unl.edu).

[Haworth co-indexing entry note]: "What a Long, Strange Trip It's Been: The Career Path of a Policy-Oriented Community Psychologist." Wilcox, Brian L. Co-published simultaneously in *Journal of Prevention & Intervention in the Community* (The Haworth Press, Inc.) Vol. 19, No. 2, 2000, pp. 83-91; and: *Employment in Community Psychology: The Diversity of Opportunity* (ed: Clifford R. O'Donnell, and Joseph R. Ferrari) The Haworth Press, Inc., 2000, pp. 83-91. Single or multiple copies of this article are available for a fee from The Haworth Document Delivery Service [1-800-342-9678, 9:00 a.m. - 5:00 p.m. (EST). E-mail address: getinfo@haworthpressinc.com].

was best described by Bandura (1974), during his Western Psychological Association Presidential Address which I attended as a college senior in 1973. Bandura recounted the important role of chance factors in the lives of a number of eminent individuals. He tells of a Nobel Prize winner whose choice of a field of study was influenced by a chance event. While in graduate school, the chemist's wife wanted to buy him a chemistry book for his birthday but could not afford any of the very expensive chemistry volumes in the college bookstore. As she was about to leave she noticed a stack of inexpensive "remaindered" books and in the stack she found a single chemistry book, which she purchased. The book's topic, boron, was unfashionable at the time, but the young chemist-to-be read it and found himself interested in some problems described in the book. His Nobel Prize was awarded for work he did on the structure of boron rings.

Most of us can recall chance events which have had important formative effects on our life choices, including our careers. There were certainly a number of such events that shaped my career choice and path. But there were many non-chance factors relating to how I got to where I am today.

Where I am today, and the path I took to get there, is not easy to describe. I am a community psychologist, one of those who was actually trained in a community psychology program–not clinical, not "community-hyphen-something-else" psychology. I currently direct the Center on Children, Families, and the Law at the University of Nebraska and teach policy-oriented courses within the developmental and law/psychology programs. But since the beginning of my graduate training I've had a very strong interest in public policy, and over the years that interest came to dominate my professional activities, from research to teaching to application.

## STUMBLING INTO PSYCHOLOGY

I wandered into psychology partly by chance. I began college with the expectation that I would major in history, although I had given little or no thought to the questions of what I might do with a history degree. I chose history primarily because I had always done well in history classes. I suspect my primary motivation was finding a major that would require the minimum amount of effort on my part while still seeming "respectable" to my parents (hence my decision not to major in physical education). My plans were altered by a terrible American history course taught by the chairperson of the History Department. In search of something different, I enrolled in an introductory psychology course taught by a professor with a reputation for being both demanding and provocative. It was the provocative aspect that appealed to me, but I soon found the "science of behavior and the mind," which is how this professor defined psychology, to be incredibly exciting. Goodbye history, hello psychology. Again, though, I wasn't really thinking about what I might do with a psychology major.

Three additional events helped give focus to my career plans. First, one of the faculty members in the Psychology Department was involved in a large research project which was focused on testing the efficacy of a behavioral psychosocial rehabilitation model in working with chronically mentally ill individuals in community settings. I was given the opportunity to work as a research assistant on the Behavioral Analysis and Modification Project run out of Camarillo State Hospital and the Oxnard Community Mental Health Center. This was my introduction to the community mental health movement. I discovered a small body of work by a group of psychologists–Iscoe, Bloom, Golann, Kelly, Spielberger, and a few others–and read everything I could find.

Second, despite my best intentions, I did well in college, and particularly in my psychology courses. Towards the end of my junior year I was asked by the Psychology Department chairman if I would be interested in serving as a departmental assistant. My school, California Lutheran College, was an undergraduate-only institution, so all assistantships went to undergraduates. I jumped at the chance, as this would allow me to work more closely with the department faculty, and I was starting to realize that graduate school might be in my future. One of those faculty, who arrived during the summer before my senior year, noted my interest in community mental health, but suggested that I might be interested in a field of psychology that was just developing: community psychology. This faculty member had just graduated from the University of Texas and, while not a community psychologist, had taken a seminar with Ira Iscoe and was very excited about this new field. So was I.

One of the reasons I became so excited about community psychology relates to the third event giving shape to my career path. Here's where chance really entered into the mix. In the summer between my junior and senior years I stayed on campus and worked for the college. At that time my college served as the summer training camp for the Dallas Cowboys, and I got a choice position working with the Cowboy coaches and business manager. Among the many tasks I was given was driving those players cut or traded from the team to the airport. This generally wasn't an enjoyable task, though I got a lot of practice using the empathic reflective listening skills I'd learned in my counseling and psychotherapy course. One particular player I drove to the airport was a highly-touted quarterback prospect. As we drove to the airport, he read a book in silence, and as I pulled up to the terminal to drop him off, he tossed the book onto the seat next to me and said, "You can have this. I thought it was about insurance." I took the book with me and began reading it that evening. The book was *Blaming the Victim* by William Ryan (1971). This book, which became required reading for every community psychologist trained in the 1970s, gave me a different frame of reference for thinking about the sorts of human problems with which I had become interested. One of the key lessons I carried away from my reading of this book was that our programs and policies are apt to contribute further to the problems they purportedly address if extra-individual factors are not taken into consideration. My view of how social problems are framed was dramatically altered. A few months later I read the now-classic Caplan and Nelson (1973) article on the nature and consequences of psychological definitions of social problems. I was convinced that community psychology, with its ecological orientation, represented a more sensible pathway to understanding and addressing social problems than did traditional clinical or social psychology.

## COMMUNITY PSYCHOLOGY:
## A FIRST FORAY INTO POLICY

Selecting a graduate program was not simple; there were few programs identified as "community psychology programs." Some "community" programs were not necessarily called community programs, such as the Transactional-Ecological Psychology Program at George Peabody College and the Ecological Program at Michigan State University, and I wasn't savvy enough to recognize these as programs that might provide the experiences I wanted. After a misstep that wasted one year of graduate training, I found myself in Austin, Texas, a student in the second class of a freestanding community psychology program at the University of Texas.

The Texas program, which sadly no longer exists in a form bearing any relationship to the program I entered, was quite unique. When I arrived the program had only two faculty members: Ira Iscoe and Charles (Josh) Holahan. To compensate for the small program faculty, Iscoe created a program which made use of the entire university. "The University is your smorgasbord," Iscoe used to say. "Go. Partake."

The program faculty taught only a handful of regular graduate courses. The meat of the program was to be found outside of the psychology department, and by the time I finished, I had as many courses outside of psychology as I had within the department. Interesting courses which fit within the model of community psychology being taught at Texas were found in all sorts of interesting places. I took a community planning course with the Community and Regional Planning Department in the Architecture School, a policy analysis course in the Social Welfare Program of the School of Social Work, courses on social intervention and theories of social change in the Sociology Department, and various other courses in educational psychology and political science.

In addition to coursework, students in the program were expected to participate in a series of 20-hour-per-week field placements beginning in their second year. Given that Austin is the state capital and the home of most state agencies, most placements were with state policy agencies. I had placements with the Texas Youth Council, the Department of Mental Health and Mental Retardation, and the Department of Community Affairs. I received my first taste of policy involvement with the Texas Youth Council, which was under court order to remove juveniles from adult facilities and to remove status offenders from their institutional programs.

Another key event in my graduate training was the relationship I developed with another graduate student, Jim Spearly. Jim came to Texas with a degree from the Yale Law School, and with Jim's encouragement, I began to look at legal and policy interventions as squarely within the purview of community psychology. Jim helped teach me both the potential and limitations of legal and policy interventions, and talked me into taking courses in the Law College and at the LBJ School of Public Affairs. Most of these courses focused on child and family policy and law. I might have remained a perpetual graduate student, given how much I enjoyed these courses, but Ira Iscoe reminded me in his direct but caring fashion that I was doing no one any good as long as I remained in graduate school.

The transition from graduate student to faculty member does not spell the end of one's education, and I was fortunate enough to find myself a member of the community psychology faculty at the University of Virginia where several faculty members had strong policy interests. Here I began teaching a regular seminar on child development and social policy, and this course became the one I genuinely looked forward to each year. Still, despite the policy courses and field placement experiences I'd had in graduate school, I felt as though I was teaching something that I didn't fully comprehend, something that was too removed from my own experience.

For some years I'd seen advertisements for the Society for Research in Child Development's Congressional Science Fellowship Program. I was intrigued, but the timing never seemed right. I finally realized that the timing would never seem just right because it was easier to keep doing what I was doing rather than undertake something that might send me off my well-laid-out path. So, of course, I applied for, and was fortunate enough to receive, an SRCD Congressional Science Fellowship.

## *DR. WILCOX GOES TO WASHINGTON*

The fellowship involved spending a year as a staff member in the office of a congressional committee or a member of Congress. After a three week intensive orientation to the world of federal policy making, I arranged to spend the year working for Sen. Bill Bradley, a Democrat from New Jersey. My choice was based on Bradley's reputation as an intelligent and effective legislator and on the quality of his professional staff. During the year I had an opportunity to view the policy-making process from the inside, and to get involved in several specific policy issues such as family and medical leave, low-income tax policy, drop-out prevention, and gifted and talented education. My intention in taking the fellowship was to add flesh to my understanding of the policy-making process and return to the University of Virginia where I would teach a more fully realized policy course. But things don't always go according to plans.

A semester after returning to Virginia, I found myself being recruited for the child and family policy position within APA's Office of Legislative Affairs. The pull of Washington, DC was strong; I had contracted Potomac Fever, and I agreed to take the position. This position, it seemed to me, was an ideal one for a community psychologist with policy leanings. My job would involve communicating policy-relevant psychological research to the legislative, executive, and judicial branches of government, and in turn educating psychologists about the opportunities for becoming involved in the policy process. I initially took the position with the intention of staying for two or three years, but by the time I left Washington, nearly nine years had passed.

The opportunities for psychologists in federal policy-making are enormous, but there are few positions labeled "psychologist" in the policy arena. Indeed, the most common reaction of colleagues to their learning I was a psychologist was, "What's a psychologist doing on Capitol Hill?" A good question, but one easily answered: many of the policies acted upon by lawmakers in all three branches of government make explicit or implicit assumptions about how those policies will affect the behavior of people or whether they will alleviate problems experienced by people. Policies promoting parental notification and consent for adolescents seeking contraceptive services or abortions are predicated in part on assumptions about adolescents' decision-making competence. Policies intending to regulate child care services make assumptions about what the critical components of child care for child well-being are. Tax and welfare policies are predicated on assumptions about what factors will serve as incentives or disincentives to labor market participation. Health care policies are created with the intent of promoting healthy lifestyles or discouraging risky behaviors, and the underlying causal implicit models often fall within the purview of psychology.

On a more practical and "nitty-gritty" level, the practice of politics within the policy making sphere calls for the skills of the community psychologist. Moving legislation forward is dependent upon the building of majorities who will support the policy proposal at various stages of the policy process. This requires the building of multiple coalitions around the policy goal, and if there is anything community psychologists should be good at, it is entering unfamiliar territory and developing relationships and partnerships intended to benefit all concerned.

While my analytic skills were very important to my work, actually getting something done (beyond educating others) was far more dependent on my ability to bring diverse groups together and help them find common ground in a way that they could move the policy process forward. Over the nearly nine years I was in Washington, there were many successes, but all of those successes came about through the efforts of many, and I can't point to a single policy outcome for which I can honestly take credit. This, of course, should sound familiar to the applied community psychologist.

## A RETURN (OF SORTS) TO THE ACADEMY

After many years I decided it was time to follow the earlier plan and return to a university where I could now teach policy courses without feeling somewhat fraudulent. Happily, I was able to come to a setting where I could continue to be engaged in the policy process. Most psychology departments don't know what to do with nontraditional psychologists, but the University of Nebraska, home of the first J.D./Ph.D. Law/Psychology program, was a welcoming place for a policy psychologist. Coincidentally, the nexus of child policy activity began shifting from Washington, DC to the states at about the time I moved to Nebraska, compliments of the Republican takeover of Congress. Thus, I find myself still in the midst of the action, but in a setting where there is (very) occasionally time to reflect on my work and even an opportunity to conduct empirical policy research and analysis. The staff at our Center on Children, Families and the Law has included several community psychologists who have, through various means, acquired legal and policy expertise to go along with their backgrounds in child welfare and children's services. My graduate students, I've found, are attracted to policy work, and many see policy involvement as a key career goal.

The path I took to policy work was circuitous and partly shaped by chance factors. But my mentors, especially Ira Iscoe, helped take my nascent policy leanings and channel them into a form that allowed me to pursue them. Training in community psychology was essential to my ability to work effectively in policy settings, but it was not sufficient. The additional experiences I received in law and policy courses elsewhere in the university, along with the experience gained by working in policy settings, was essential to understanding the community, or culture, of policy-makers. Fortunately, these are experiences nearly any student can pursue in a graduate program that is flexible enough to allow students to make use of the whole university. Policy work isn't for the meek; the process can be ugly. It is not for those who feel the need to exert control over their agenda; the process is unpredictable. And it's not for those who want to see results right away; the process can drag on for years and decades. But if one has a tolerance for ambiguity and a feel for politics, applied policy work is a reasonable career option for the community psychologist.

## REFERENCES

Bandura, A. (1982). The psychology of chance encounters and life paths. *American Psychologist, 32,* 747-755.

Caplan, N., & Nelson, S. (1973). On being useful: The nature and consequences of psychological research on social problems. *American Psychologist, 28,* 199-211.

Ryan, W. (1971). *Blaming the victim.* New York: Random House.

# Employment as a Community Psychologist in a University-Based Research Institute

Kurt M. Ribisl

Stanford University School of Medicine

**SUMMARY.** The present paper describes the educational background and current role of a community psychologist conducting tobacco control studies at a research institute affiliated with a university medical school. This includes how the author originally became interested in community psychology as an undergraduate, chose a graduate training program and postdoctoral fellowship, and how this training was instrumental in obtaining the current position. *[Article copies available for a fee from The Haworth Document Delivery Service: 1-800-342-9678. E-mail address: getinfo@haworthpressinc.com <Website: http://www.haworthpressinc.com>]*

**KEYWORDS.** Community psychology, public policy, health promotion

I work in a multidisciplinary team at Stanford University that conducts community intervention studies to reduce tobacco use, primarily among youth. My other colleagues are a nurse, a physician, a biostatistician, a social psychologist, and experts in public health and communication. We study how the tobacco industry markets their products toward youth and how youth obtain tobacco products from both retail

Address correspondence to: Kurt M. Ribisl, Stanford Center for Research in Disease Prevention, Stanford University School of Medicine, 1000 Welch Road, Palo Alto, CA 94304-1825.

[Haworth co-indexing entry note]: "Employment as a Community Psychologist in a University-Based Research Institute." Ribisl, Kurt M. Co-published simultaneously in *Journal of Prevention & Intervention in the Community* (The Haworth Press, Inc.) Vol. 19, No. 2, 2000, pp. 93-100; and: *Employment in Community Psychology: The Diversity of Opportunity* (ed: Clifford R. O'Donnell, and Joseph R. Ferrari) The Haworth Press, Inc., 2000, pp. 93-100. Single or multiple copies of this article are available for a fee from The Haworth Document Delivery Service [1-800-342-9678, 9:00 a.m. - 5:00 p.m. (EST). E-mail address: getinfo@haworthpressinc.com].

(stores) and social (friends, relatives) sources. The goal of these efforts is to understand and expose tobacco advertising aimed at youth, reduce youth access to tobacco, and conduct policy-related research studies. Earlier, my colleagues had conducted research that was cited in the 1994 Surgeon General's report on *Tobacco Use Among Young People* and the recent FDA regulations governing the distribution and advertising of tobacco. This is exciting work given the high profile of various tobacco issues, such as the lawsuits against the industry, proposed government restrictions on advertising and youth access, and the possibility of national tobacco legislation.

As with all positions that are funded by grants and contracts (i.e., "soft money"), I work on multiple projects. It is typical to be working on three to five research studies while also writing a grant application. In one of our current studies, we are examining the number and types of tobacco advertisements at retail outlets in a random sample of California stores. We are assessing whether advertisements are strategically placed to appeal to youth and how the number of advertisements changes over time. We are also in the midst of evaluating an intervention delivered in three communities to prevent merchants from selling tobacco to minors by using low-cost print materials based on deterrence theory. Our studies of law enforcement have shown that the primary reason they do not address the problem of illegal tobacco sales to minors is that they report having few resources to address this issue. Thus, this approach is specifically designed to rely upon minimal staff effort and low-cost materials.

Our newest venture is in addressing *social* sources of tobacco. California has already launched aggressive efforts to prevent youth from getting access to tobacco products from *retail* sources, which has led to impressive reductions in the rate of illegal tobacco sales to minors. However, teen smoking rates continue to remain high, probably because youth are now less likely to purchase their own cigarettes and are more likely to obtain them from friends and family. Our goal is to alter community norms around the practice of providing cigarettes to minors by administering interventions delivered in schools, workplaces, and via mass media. Because all of our studies occur in the community, as opposed to university laboratories, having been trained in community psychology has been a real asset to this work.

## HOW I BECAME INTERESTED
## IN COMMUNITY PSYCHOLOGY

I did not know that the field of community psychology even existed until my junior year of college. While waiting for a tardy professor, I was thumbing through some of the unassigned sections of our text in clinical psychology (Phares, 1988). There was a chapter on community psychology that immediately grabbed my attention. It talked about the benefits of focusing on prevention rather than cure, working with disenfranchised populations instead of affluent ones, and conducting community-based interventions as opposed to one-on-one encounters. Overall, this chapter encapsulated what I had been looking for all along and stimulated my interest in getting training in community psychology instead of clinical psychology. My primary concern, however, was the legitimacy and durability of the field. After all, the university did not offer any classes in community psychology, I had never seen or met a community psychologist, and the community psychology chapter was not even assigned. Perhaps community psychology was really a fringe activity–the lesser known and eccentric cousin of clinical psychology. Thus, I was very ambivalent–should I venture out into this area, which by psychology's standard was a relative newcomer born around 30 years ago?

As a psychology major, my interest was in health promotion, particularly health promotion in workplace and community settings. To cover all of my bases, I applied to three types of psychology programs: clinical health psychology, clinical-community programs, and stand-alone community programs. I applied to a total of eight programs and was accepted at one clinical, one clinical-community, and one community program. To explore these options, I sacrificed a trip to the beach with my roommates during Spring Break and chose instead to visit the three snow-covered Midwestern schools that accepted me. My choice was quickly narrowed to either the clinical-community or the stand-alone community program, but I was still torn between them. My hunch that I was not destined for the "clinical" in clinical-community was confirmed by my undergraduate advisor. She kindly, but bluntly, confessed that I did not really have the disposition to be a clinical psychologist because I would be frustrated always dealing with other people's problems. She was painfully right about my quickly fading empathy skills–I felt that I possessed a good listening ear for the short-term problems that afflicted my friends, but I quickly became bored with their recurring personal issues. In addition, taking years of classes in clinical topics such as assessment and therapy did not make sense if I only really cared about developing community intervention skills. It was decided–I chose to enroll in the Ecological-Community Psychology Program at Michigan State University (MSU).

## GRADUATE SCHOOL EXPERIENCES

One of the most exciting aspects of the graduate program at MSU was the applied focus on pressing social issues such as homelessness, juvenile delinquency, mental illness, and violence against women. Moreover, there was rigorous evaluation of alternative solutions to addressing these vexing social problems. The program forced you to study real people in real communities experiencing real problems in their daily lives. Unlike my other friends attending graduate school in psychology, I was certain that I would not be studying rats or under-graduates at any point in this program. The professors also nudged us into the community right away. In fact, I was practically knocking on doors trying to find an internship for my practicum class before I had memorized my new phone number. Shortly thereafter, I attended a conference on health promotion issues where I met a man at the happy hour who worked at the Michigan Department of Public Health (MDPH). He was in charge of an innovative program that offered health promotion grants to small workplaces. I offered to work for free as an intern at MDPH as part of my practicum requirement and this offer was accepted. Eventually, I recruited workplaces for my master's thesis through organizations that had received health promotion grants.

To pay for my tuition at MSU, I was a Teaching Assistant (TA) for my first year. The next year, I became a Research Assistant (RA) on a program evaluation study of an innovative treatment program for people with dual psychiatric and drug abuse problems. I did my dissertation on the role of social networks in predicting recovery from substance abuse problems. This topic incorporated many of the core values of community psychology, such as focusing on a person's strengths (i.e., how their social network bonds may promote sobriety), working with a disenfranchised population, and taking into account social and contextual factors predicting relapse instead of just treatment and intrapsychic factors. While completing this study, an interesting job opportunity presented itself at MDPH during my fourth year of graduate school. I could be employed within the same division I originally interned at, and I could help direct a telephone study of the alcohol and drug use of 7,000 Michigan adults. I accepted this new position because it would provide new learning opportunities in epidemiology and how to conduct population studies. As a result of this position, I learned two very important things, namely: (1) how to conduct and analyze data from a large-scale population survey; and (2) that I would never want to work for the state (and probably federal) government. I just did not have the temperament or patience to survive working in a politically-laden government bureaucracy. As I was finishing my dissertation, I then had to make a decision about my next career move.

## A POSTDOC OR AN ACADEMIC TEACHING JOB?

My ultimate career goal since being an undergraduate has been to be a professor at a university that values both teaching and research. I felt I had two options after graduate school: directly applying for teaching positions or for postdoctoral research fellowships (i.e., postdocs) followed by seeking an academic position. One of my dissertation committee members told me I was foolish for considering a postdoc because the pay was terrible and I could learn "on the job" anyway as an assistant professor. On the other hand, in the area of health psychology and disease prevention it was becoming increasingly common to do a two or three year postdoc. In any case, I decided to be picky in my job search and I applied for only three academic jobs at places that seemed appropriate given my interests in health, but that were also in desirable geographical locations. In addition, I applied to two postdocs. One of the postdocs was at the Stanford Center for Research in Disease Prevention (SCRDP), which is part of the university's medical school. I applied to SCRDP because during a recent conference I had met a community psychologist who was doing interesting work in the area of tobacco control. It was a chance meeting when I nervously approached him at the health psychology "happy hour" to ask about his work. He encouraged me to consider applying to their postdoc because the group valued the skills of community psychologists. These skills included knowledge about developing and evaluating community interventions, being sensitive to diversity issues, and focusing on methods to make community-level changes instead of just changing individuals' health behaviors. My interest in the Stanford postdoc also increased after I met the department chair at a school of public health at a different conference. I proudly told him that I had applied for their advertised assistant professor position. As we talked further, I also mentioned applying for the postdoc at Stanford with the group doing community intervention studies. He said that there was no question in his mind that I should spend the time doing a postdoc and then later on apply for an academic position.

Deciding between the postdoc or an academic job was quite easy due to the fact that I was rejected at all three places for the teaching job. However, I was accepted at two postdocs and easily chose the one at SCRDP. The group that I would be working with was known for conducting two ground-breaking community-based cardiovascular risk reduction interventions, the Stanford Three Community Study (Farquhar et al., 1977) and the Stanford Five-City Project (Farquhar et al., 1990). I have written about the pros and cons of doing a postdoc in another article (Ribisl, 1995), so I will not go into that any further here. In retrospect, doing the postdoc was definitely the right choice because I was able to learn new ways of thinking about community interventions, and I was able to learn more about epidemiological research methods and statistics. As I reflect back on my graduate training in community psychology, I believe that there were three primary reasons why I was selected to do the postdoc at Stanford.

First, the SCRDP faculty definitely valued the community psychology training that I had received. For instance, I would regularly rely on my training to gain entry and acceptance into the communities where we conducted our studies. This includes ensuring that the community will benefit from the research, that its strengths are maximized, and having an understanding that is takes ample time to build a relationship with the community or to repair one previously fractured by other investigators. This was important because each day we deal with diverse groups such as police officers, school principals, tobacco merchants, teenagers and their parents. My training also taught me about dealing with the unique statistical and design challenges encountered in real world settings, which are not encountered in more controlled, but artificial, laboratory studies. Many people would agree that the training in quantitative methods and research design in psychology or the behavioral sciences far exceeds that of most other disciplines.

Besides solid community training, the second reason I was suitable for the postdoc was that I had research experience in two different settings: the public psychiatric hospital and the Department of Public Health. Finally, the third reason was that I had some experience with publishing as a graduate student. When my advisors learned of my desire for an academic position, they strongly urged me to work as soon as possible on scientific manuscripts. In my second year, for instance, I was invited to write a book chapter with one professor, and in my third year I published my master's thesis with another professor. I also had submitted several manuscripts from the research project at the psychiatric hospital. Thus, students seeking postdocs or faculty positions should talk with their advisors not only about opportunities for publishing their master's thesis and dissertation, but also about working on other ongoing projects that can lead to valuable research experience and publications.

## CONCLUSION

The pace at any research institute that relies on soft-money is intense because of the constant need to write enough research grants to support yourself and your staff. Getting grants is harder now than in the past because the funding rates are lower, and getting a grant funded by the National Institutes of Health now often requires submitting it two or three times. Nevertheless, there are great advantages to working at a research institute because you are often working with individuals who are very well known in their fields, who form a cohesive multidisciplinary team, and you are able to conduct research that has long-term socially significant implications. However, my ultimate goal is to enter academics doing both teaching and research, instead of being a full-time researcher. Also, having a secure, hard-money income is more reassuring than knowing that your position is only contingent upon grant funding. For these reasons along with a desire to teach, I plan on seeking an academic job in a few years. I was glad that I did the postdoc and worked at a research institute dedicated to preventing disease and promoting health. Overall, I realize how chance encounters can greatly influence your life and job plans. Therefore, when I attend conferences I am committed to always attending the happy hour.

# REFERENCES

Farquhar, J. W., Fortmann, S. P., Flora, J. A., Taylor, C. B., Haskell, W. L., Williams, P. T., Maccoby, N., & Wood, P. D. (1990 (aux)). Effects of communitywide education on cardiovascular disease risk factors (auxilliary document). *Journal of the American Medical Association, 264,* 359-365.

Farquhar, J. W., Wood, P. D., Breitrose, H., Alexander, J. K., Breitrose, H., Brown, B. W. J., Haskell, W. L., McAlister, A. L., Meyer, A. J., Nash, J. D., & Stern, M. P. (1977). Community education for cardiovascular health. *Lancet, 1,* 1192-1195.

Phares, E. J. (1988). Community Psychology. In *Clinical psychology: Concepts, methods, and profession* (pp. 486-523). Chicago: Dorsey Press.

Ribisl, K. M. (1995). Should you consider doing a postdoc after graduate school? *The Community Psychologist, 28*(5), 31-33.

# Building Communities
# with People Who Have Disabilities

## Dale R. Fryxell

University of Hawaii

**SUMMARY.** Many community psychologists have the educational and professional backgrounds which make them potentially valuable resources for the disabilities field. The Americans with Disabilities Act of 1990 (ADA) and the reauthorized Individuals with Disabilities Education Act (IDEA) call for greater community inclusion, empowerment, and self-determination for persons with disabilities. Community psychologists with interests in these concepts, as well as in interdisciplinary training, collaboration, community-driven research, and political action are needed as leaders in the disabilities field. This paper explores the development of one community psychologist's career working with persons who have disabilities and the institutions that support them. *[Article copies available for a fee from The Haworth Document Delivery Service: 1-800-342-9678. E-mail address: getinfo@haworthpressinc. com <Website: http://www.haworthpressinc.com>]*

**KEYWORDS.** Community psychology, disabilities

The disabilities field provides an exciting and challenging specialization area where the knowledge and skills related to community psychology are greatly needed. Many opportunities are available for

---

Address correspondence to: Dale R. Fryxell, Hawaii University Affiliated Program, University of Hawaii, 1776 University Avenue, UA4-6, Honolulu, HI 96822.

[Haworth co-indexing entry note]: "Building Communities with People Who Have Disabilities." Fryxell, Dale R. Co-published simultaneously in *Journal of Prevention & Intervention in the Community* (The Haworth Press, Inc.) Vol. 19, No. 2, 2000, pp. 101-108; and: *Employment in Community Psychology: The Diversity of Opportunity* (ed: Clifford R. O'Donnell, and Joseph R. Ferrari) The Haworth Press, Inc., 2000, pp. 101-108. Single or multiple copies of this article are available for a fee from The Haworth Document Delivery Service [1-800-342-9678, 9:00 a.m. - 5:00 p.m. (EST). E-mail address: getinfo@haworthpressinc.com].

*101*

community psychologists in programs similar to those of my current position as the project coordinator for a federally funded project at the Hawaii University Affiliated Program within the University of Hawaii. There are University Affiliated Programs (UAP) in all 50 states and several Pacific island jurisdictions. The UAPs were set up to provide research, training, and the dissemination of information related to the disabilities field. The Hawaii UAP has projects that serve populations from prenatal through the aging developmental periods and include medical, educational, and social service components. The project I coordinate, "The Positive Behavioral Support Training Initiative," is funded through a grant accepted during the final year of my doctoral program in community psychology. It incorporates many of the theories and methodologies from community psychology into a comprehensive program designed to support individuals who have developed challenging or severe behavior problems. The goals of this project are to provide training and consultation to interdisciplinary teams from schools, adult day programs for people with disabilities, community organizations, and to the Hawaii State Department of Health-Developmental Disabilities Division. Most of these interdisciplinary teams are struggling with funding cuts and case load increases to provide support to individuals who display aggressive, violent, or self-injurious behaviors. A major emphasis of this project is to assist the state in closing of the state's only institution for persons with developmental disabilities, Waimano Home and Training School. Many of the hundreds of people once institutionalized there need support to develop and maintain a high quality of life in their new community settings.

The positive behavioral support training model that has been developed in Hawaii and in several other states combines an interdisciplinary and collaborative team-building approach to support individuals. This model is unique in that it has moved away from strict behavior modification principles and takes on a more environmental and person-centered approach for supporting people with challenging behaviors. The model views behavior as a form of communication that needs to be understood before it can be changed. Tools such as functional behavior analysis and futures planning are used to develop comprehensive behavioral support plans that are based on personal strengths rather than deficits and are geared towards meeting the unique needs of each individual.

Recently, services have been extended to several school districts who are interested in providing support to students in kindergarten through second grade who are at risk for developing more severe future behavior problems or who could be referred for special education services if they don't get the support they need. Some of these students are just having trouble adjusting to a school environment, others are having academic difficulties, and some are engaging in more serious behaviors that could have long term consequences.

Since completing my Ph.D. in August of 1997, in addition to coordinating the Positive Behavioral Supports Training Initiative grant, I have been selected as one of the five initiative leaders for the Hawaii UAP. My responsibilities as the leader for the School and Community Inclusion Initiative include representing the initiative in meetings, developing new grant proposals, and disseminating and collecting information to and from the other initiative members. I have also recently been appointed as the Chair of the Hawaii UAP's Executive Council. This council is responsible for providing direction for the UAP, for providing individual and grant specific support, and serves as a link between the UAP and the larger university and community.

The story of my involvement in community psychology and the disabilities field is an interesting one and one never imagined 15 years ago as the owner of a small commercial furniture design and construction business. It all started when my wife and I decided that we would like to try something new and have some adventure. We decided to join the Peace Corps! Off we went to the Republic of Kiribati (a small island country in the Central Pacific), where we worked with "Save the Children." It was here that my interest and passion for community development work was sparked. My time in the Peace Corps involved organizing community groups, building water catchment and distribution systems, and experimenting with assistive technologies (smokeless stoves, food preservation, solar power, etc.). Working with community groups to help them form cohesive units that could work together to learn new skills, gather resources, and improve not only their own lives, but the lives of all those in their communities was also part of my job. After two great years in the Peace Corps, I returned to Minnesota, completed an undergraduate degree in sociology and a Master's degree in education. My next goal was to pursue a doctoral degree leading to a profession that would include teaching, community development, and improving physical and mental health for at risk populations. The problem was trying to find a field of study that would encompass all of these factors.

The answer came in a Peace Corps publication that advertised graduate programs that may be of interest to returned volunteers. One of the programs listed was a doctoral program in community psychology at the University of Hawaii. The program described a community psychology program that incorporated many of my personal and professional interests. In addition, the thought of leaving the frozen midwest for Hawaii seemed appealing. So we packed up our two young children, twenty-five boxes and off we went.

The Director of the Community Psychology Program at the University of Hawaii (Dr. Cliff O'Donnell) lined up a graduate assistant position for me with the Hawaii University Affiliated Program, which according to some literature had something to do with developmental disabilities. Little did I know that this chance happening would lead to an interest and career working with people who have disabilities. After all, up to this point, my only knowledge about this group had been learned from the few fleeting glimpses of special education students while in elementary school and some volunteer work done for Special Olympics as a teenager.

Upon my arrival in Hawaii in the Fall, 1992, I started the community psychology program and began working as a graduate assistant on the Statewide Systems Change Project for Students with Severe Disabilities. The purpose of this federally-funded project was to collaborate with the Department of Education in the State of Hawaii, to make systemic changes that would result in improvements in the educational opportunities and outcomes for students who receive special education services. This graduate assistant job turned out to be a stepping stone for me that led to many great opportunities, including my current position. In addition, my work at the Hawaii UAP proved to be an ideal fit with many of the concepts and principles learned as part of my coursework in the community psychology program. These concepts and principles included community development, empowerment, social supports and social networks, interdisciplinary collaboration, self help, advocacy, and legislative reform. During this period, I signed on as a trainee in the developmental disabilities certificate program conducted by the Hawaii UAP. This program involved taking several disability-related courses which complimented my community psychology program with the added bonus of tuition and stipend support.

After only nine months as a graduate assistant, I was promoted to a full-time position as the inservice coordinator for the project. While in this position, there were many great opportunities to conduct workshops and teacher inservices on a wide variety of topics including: team building, collaboration, inclusive education, effective teaching strategies, building social supports, systems change, school reform, and behavior support techniques. Within four months of taking the Inservice Coordinator position, the Project Coordinator left Hawaii to take a new position and I was in line to take over the project as the new coordinator. My responsibilities now encompassed running a federal grant with a half million dollar budget and five staff members. My work over the next two years involved conducting training, working on systemic change, and providing consultation. Additionally, there was the opportunity to implement many of the ideas and concepts learned in the community psychology program into project activities.

One of the important new skills developed during this period was in the area of grant writing. Participation on grant writing teams with several experienced and successful grant writers at the Hawaii UAP was expected of all new faculty members. The Hawaii UAP and almost all of the people that work there are funded by state and federal grants for a specific period of time. It was very clear that being a successful grant writer was important if one wanted to continue working in this environment.

After the Statewide Systems Change Project ended, I worked half-time on each of two projects. The first project was with the Department of Special Education at the University of Hawaii, on a federally funded research project investigating the social networks and social supports available to middle school students with severe disabilities who were included in regular education programs (Fryxell & Kennedy, 1996; Kennedy, Shukla, & Fryxell, 1997). The research that we conducted for this project was very similar to and an extension of prior research done for my Master's thesis the previous year. My Master's thesis (Fryxell, 1995) compared the social networks and social supports available to elementary aged students who were either included or excluded from regular education classes.

The second project involved serving as the coordinator for the Minority Assistance Institute project (MAI) at the Hawaii UAP. This federally funded program had been designed to recruit minority under-graduate students who were interested in pursuing a health career and would like to work toward a certificate in developmental disabilities. My work on this project helped me to examine, in depth, many of the racial and cultural issues that were becoming familiar themes within my community psychology coursework. Providing academic and career counseling to students enrolled in this program proved to be both rewarding and enjoyable.

During this period, I continued to take an active role in the community psychology program where I served as the student representative to Division 27 of the American Psychology Association, the Society for Community Research and Action. After completing the certificate program in developmental disabilities, I was selected as the health administration trainee in the Maternal Child Health Leadership Education in Neurodevelopmental Disabilities Program. This year-long program provided an excellent opportunity to not only learn more about disabilities and the people and families that have them, but also gave me a chance to work collaboratively with students and professors from other health related programs including medicine, nursing, occupational and physical therapy, nutrition, social work, clinical psychology, and speech/audiology. This unique program, a collaborative effort between the Hawaii UAP and the John A. Burns School of Medicine, paired one student and one faculty member from each discipline to come together weekly to explore the physical, mental, social, and political aspects of disabilities.

Since aggressive and challenging behaviors had become a major personal and professional interest of mine, a decision was made to conduct my dissertation on factors related to the development of anger, a component which seems to underlie many of the behaviors I was witnessing (Fryxell, 1997). My dissertation used both qualitative and quantitative methods to examine the factors that put children at risk for developing extreme angry feelings, aggressive behaviors, or hostile thoughts. This research was conducted with 5th and 6th grade regular and special education students at three public elementary schools in the State of Hawaii. The study involved conducting extensive interviews with students, teachers, and parents as well as administering several assessment instruments. The results of the study indicated that certain risk factors associated with four developmental domains; individual personality and temperament, family environment, school environment, and peer and social interactions were significantly related to anger, aggression, and hostility.

While working on these projects and completing my own course-work, I was also busy gaining valuable teaching experience. During my second year in the community psychology program, the opportunity to teach undergraduate courses for the psychology department was made available to me. Prior to completing my Ph.D. during the summer of 1997, I had taught over twenty undergraduate psychology courses including community psychology, developmental psychology, social psychology, organizational psychology, and abnormal psychology. The development of a relationship with the Family Resources Department led to additional opportunities to teach human development courses for this department. In addition to teaching undergraduate courses, opportunities opened up to began teaching graduate courses for the Master's in Counseling Psychology Program at Chaminade University.

In conclusion, I would advise and encourage future community psychologists to explore the disabilities field as an exciting and growing field in need of trained professionals who can provide leadership in the areas of research, dissemination, consultation, and training. I would also advise future professionals to take advantage of as many and as varied opportunities as possible as part of your graduate training. These opportunities may include interdisciplinary training, teaching, conducting research, and experiencing various internships and practicum opportunities. My work in the disabilities field with the Hawaii University Affiliated program has provided me with many opportunities for professional development including: funding to attend and present at major national conferences; support for writing grant proposals to both public and private agencies; support for conducting research; and opportunities for leadership. I look forward to using my community psychology background to continue educating the public about disabilities, working for the empowerment of persons with disabilities and their families, and working to improve the quality of life for this population. The disability field has many opportunities for dedicated professionals and is a great area to practice community research and action!

## REFERENCES

Fryxell, D. R. (1997). *Risk factors associated with chronic anger, hostility, and aggression in preadolescent youth.* Unpublished doctoral dissertation, University of Hawaii, Manoa.

Fryxell, D., & Kennedy, C. (1996). Placement along the continuum of services and its impact on students' social relationships. *Journal of the Association for Persons with Severe Handicaps, 20*(4), 259-269.

Fryxell, D. R. (1995). *The effects of inclusive education on friendship, social networks, and social support for elementary-aged students with severe disabilities.* Unpublished thesis, University of Hawaii, Manoa.

Kennedy, C. H., Shukla, S. & Fryxell, D. (1997). Comparing the effects of educational placement on the social relationships of intermediate school students with severe disabilities. *Exceptional Children, 64*(1), 31-47.

# Breaking Fresh Ground:
# School-Based Primary Prevention in Korea

## HyunHee Chung

Korea Institute of Social Psychiatry

**ABSTRACT.** In the present paper, the author introduces her roles and duties at her current job. The author then describes how she got into community psychology and primary prevention and how her graduate school and previous work experiences have influenced her current work. Focusing on primary prevention, the author delineates how the two community psychology concepts–primary prevention and action research–can be applied to the promotion of adolescent mental health in the Korean society. The author then adds advice for foreign students who are considering studying community psychology in the U.S. *[Article copies available for a fee from The Haworth Document Delivery Service: 1-800-342-9678. E-mail address: getinfo@haworthpressinc.com <Website: http://www.haworthpressinc.com>]*

**KEYWORDS.** Community psychology, primary prevention, school psychology

Since 1996, I have been working as a researcher at the Korea Institute of Social Psychiatry (KISP). KISP is a private research institute with an aim to promote the mental health of Korean people. KISP

---

Address correspondence to: HyunHee Chung, Korea Institute of Social Psychiatry, Sansung Life, 26th Floor, 150 Taepyungro 2GA, Choong-Ku, Seoul, Korea.

[Haworth co-indexing entry note]: "Breaking Fresh Ground: School-Based Primary Prevention in Korea." Chung, HyunHee. Co-published simultaneously in *Journal of Prevention & Intervention in the Community* (The Haworth Press, Inc.) Vol. 19, No. 2, 2000, pp. 109-114; and: *Employment in Community Psychology: The Diversity of Opportunity* (ed: Clifford R. O'Donnell, and Joseph R. Ferrari) The Haworth Press, Inc., 2000, pp. 109-114. Single or multiple copies of this article are available for a fee from The Haworth Document Delivery Service [1-800-342-9678, 9:00 a.m. - 5:00 p.m. (EST). E-mail address: getinfo@haworthpressinc.com].

is a multidisciplinary setting composed of professionals with various training backgrounds (e.g., psychology, psychiatry, sociology, education, and social work). I think this makes KISP a unique, attractive place for the Korean researchers who are interested in studying and improving the mental health of people. This is especially true for psychologists, given that there are not many research institutes at which a psychologist can work. Furthermore, KISP is one of the few places in Korea, where community psychology can actually be applied and practiced. For this reason, I feel very fortunate to have this opportunity to work at the Institute.

My interest in this position began when I returned to Korea after I had spent seven years in the U.S. for my doctorate. Although Korea was my home country, coming back to Korea was not an easy transition. The most difficult thing for me, especially as a school psychologist, was that the Korean school systems were so different that I could not immediately apply what I had learned in the U.S. Although I had anticipated that I might face this challenge, I became quite frustrated in figuring out how to start my career. Since most doctoral-level psychologists are expected to pursue academic careers at colleges or universities, I started my career with teaching psychology courses at a university in Seoul.

While I was teaching, I happened to learn that KISP was about to be opened and was looking for a psychologist who had a background in studying adolescent mental health. Initially, I was not thrilled with applying to this position. I had not given much thought to the idea of working at a research institute. However, as I learned more about KISP, especially its mission and plans, I soon became interested in working there. I felt that my training background as a school psychologist and my research experience fit nicely with the position. I also felt that I could contribute to promoting the mental health of Korean adolescents by applying community psychology concepts to my work there. I decided to apply and obtained the position.

KISP is primarily a research institute. Thus, most of my activities at the Institute have been research-related. I do not have a problem with this, because I enjoy and feel comfortable with my role as a researcher. For the past two years, I have participated in many interesting research projects such as parent-child relationships and adolescent mental health, development of assessment tools for adolescent mental health, school environment and adolescent mental health, impact of peer victimization on adolescent mental health, etc. Currently, I am participating in a study on how Korean people are coping with the nation's present economic crisis.

In addition to data-based, quantitative research, I have also been able to get involved with an exciting action research project. Called "School Mental Health Programs for Middle School Students," this project aims to develop a three-year curriculum which can be implemented in the classroom to promote students' social competence and mental health. Like other projects at KISP, it is a multidisciplinary team project where all the team members from different disciplines (e.g., psychology, socialwork, and education) collaborate with one another. This project is a typical action research project that goes through three stages–program development, program implementation, and program evaluation. Among many activities that I have been involved with at KISP so far, I value this project the most because I feel that this is what I can contribute the most to the Korean society as a school-community psychologist.

My first contact with community psychology was through a theoretical foundations of systems approach class that I took in my second semester at Rutgers University (NJ). During this class, I was exposed to many important concepts and theories in community psychology. Among those concepts and theories, I was especially influenced by the ecological model which emphasizes the interactions of persons and their environments. This framework widened my vision and helped me understand complex human behavior from a broader perspective.

Although this class had a significant impact on me, what had eventually guided me into the field of community psychology was the ISA-SPS (Improving Social Awareness-Social Problem Solving) project. The ISA-SPS was a school-based primary prevention project jointly conducted by Rutgers University and the University of Medicine and Dentistry of New Jersey. Initially, my main duties were statistical analysis and data management. As I continued to work for the project, however, I became interested in learning more about community psychology. So, I took another community psychology class in my second year at Rutgers University. This class equipped me with a theoretical and practical knowledge basis of community psychology.

While I was working for the ISA-SPS project, I conducted a couple of other research projects that were later published. One of them was a study on the patterns of adolescent problem behavior involvement and their relationship with self-efficacy, social competence, and life events (Chung & Elias, 1996). The other project was a longitudinal study on the impact of middle school transition on adolescents' adjustment (Chung, Elias, & Schneider, 1998). These studies, together with the ISA-SPS project, provided me with a good opportunity to learn how community psychology research can occur in action.

My interest in primary prevention grew somewhat slowly. Although I had worked for the ISA-SPS project for several years, it was not until my internship year that I became seriously aware of how important and valuable primary prevention could be. After I finished all the coursework and practicum requirements at Rutgers University, I went on a pre-doctoral internship to the Children's Village (CV) in Dobbs Ferry, New York. CV was a residential treatment center for children with severe conduct and emotional problems. There, I engaged mostly in therapy and assessment as an intern. Although working with those kids was quite challenging, I worked hard thinking that I could help them and have a significant impact on their lives. However, soon I began to feel helpless and frustrated as a therapist. The problems of the children at CV were so severe that a couple of therapy sessions per week did not seem to do much for them. The harder I tried, the stronger I felt that it was too late to change them and that there was nothing much I could do to help them with their problems. It felt just like a Korean saying, "Locking the stable door after the horse was stolen." My experience at CV led me to re-evaluate the value of preventive efforts and led me more into primary prevention.

My interest in primary prevention continued to grow at my next job. After I had finished my internship at CV, I found a school psychologist position at a public school in Northern New Jersey. My main duties were pretty much what most other school psychologists would do in the schools–testing and eligibility determination for special education services. While I worked there, I noticed that the number of referrals was increasing. The administrators and teachers wanted my team to label more and more kids and to refer them out of their school. As I was carrying out my duties as a school psychologist, I began to feel very uncomfortable with my role–classification and placement. I saw many children and their parents unhappy about being classified and placed in special programs, and I felt I was not doing the right thing for them. This made me ask myself, "What would be better ways to serve these children and their families? What can be done to prevent their problem from occurring in the first place?" As I tried to answer these questions, I could see clearly the meaning and value of primary prevention.

Primary prevention is still a novel concept in Korea. But I strongly feel that it can be a very useful intervention method for Korean children and adolescents, especially in the school settings. Korean schools are now faced with various students' problems such as school violence, substance abuse, depression, suicide, etc. However, these problems are often neglected by teachers and administrators due to their ignorance and lack of awareness. In addition, there are few mental health professionals that students can go to for help in the schools. So, it is usually the parents' responsibility to take care of their children's problems. To make things even worse, however, Korean parents generally have strong resistance to utilizing mental health services. They prefer solving their children's problems within their family. This can create even more problems, leaving many children untreated.

Given these circumstances, I believe that school-based primary prevention programs can make an important contribution to promoting the mental health of Korean adolescents. My two and a half-year experience of running a project, School Mental Health Programs for Middle School Students, has led me to believe that school-based primary prevention is a valuable and promising work to do as a a school-community psychologist in Korea. But I have also learned, through many painful lessons, that conducting action research in the school is a tough business. Designing effective, user-friendly programs, getting teachers and parents involved, collaborating with other professionals, and empowering the participants, developing effective tools for program evaluation are just a few examples among many isssues that I have had to struggle with. I know that, as I go on, there will be even more challenges that I should struggle with. But I also know that I can eventually achieve the goals, as long as I continue to make "baby steps"(Cowen, 1980).

I hope this article was helpful to those who are interested in learning how community psychology principles, particularly primary prevention and action research, can be applied in a different culture. I also hope my experiences are helpful to those who are planning to study community psychology, especially to foreign students. Before closing,

I would like to offer speical advice to the foreign students who are considering studying community psychology in the U.S. "Go for it! But go with open and positive mind. Don't be afraid of challenges. Challenge will guide you to reach your goals."

## REFERENCES

Chung, H., Elias, M., & Schneider (1998). Patterns of individual adjustment changes during middle school transition. *Journal of School Psychology, 36,* 83-101.

Chung, H., & Elias, M. (1996). Patterns of adolescent involvement in problem behaviors: Relationship to self-efficacy, social competence, and life events. *American Jouranl of Community Psychology, 24,* 771-784.

Cowen, E. L. (1980). The wooking of primary prevention. *American Journal of Community Psychology, 8,* 258-284.

# Putting a Toe in the Water

## David Henry

University of Illinois at Chicago

**SUMMARY.** This article describes the author's experience entering a second career in community psychology in mid-life. The issues relating the author's first career and community psychology are discussed, as are his current activities, interests and reflections. *[Article copies available for a fee from The Haworth Document Delivery Service: 1-800-342-9678. E-mail address: getinfo@haworthpressinc.com <Website: http://www.haworthpressinc.com>]*

**KEYWORDS.** Community psychology, juvenile deliquency

"If I flunk this, I will forget grad school," I promised myself as I stood in line to enroll for a summer statistics course 14 years ago. I had scrupulously avoided statistics throughout college, but as I prepared to undertake graduate study in community psychology, avoidance was no longer an option. Remembering an ancient rabbinic legend that the sea opened when Moses put his toe in the water, I enrolled.

I undertook a master's program in clinical psychology in mid-life, after serving as a pastor in an inner-city church for nearly 10 years. Although I enjoyed my work, I had been interested in psychological research since college, and had long desired to do graduate study in psychology. One summer, once my children had attained school age, I

---

Address correspondence to: David Henry, Institute for Juvenile Research, Department of Psychiatry, 907 South Wolcott Avenue, Chicago, IL 60612.

[Haworth co-indexing entry note]: "Putting a Toe in the Water." Henry, David. Co-published simultaneously in *Journal of Prevention & Intervention in the Community* (The Haworth Press, Inc.) Vol. 19, No. 2, 2000, pp. 115-119; and: *Employment in Community Psychology: The Diversity of Opportunity* (ed: Clifford R. O'Donnell, and Joseph R. Ferrari) The Haworth Press, Inc., 2000, pp. 115-119. Single or multiple copies of this article are available for a fee from The Haworth Document Delivery Service [1-800-342-9678, 9:00 a.m. - 5:00 p.m. (EST). E-mail address: getinfo@haworthpressinc.com].

took what seemed to be a giant step, as I had been out of school for some time. I enrolled in a statistics course. I not only passed the course, but loved it, and took every statistics and research course I could manage. I have taught statistics at both undergraduate and graduate levels many times since, and frequently share this story for the benefit of those who are fearful.

Growing up, and as a young adult, I learned first-hand about the effects of ecological factors on human development and psychological health. I participated in the civil rights movement through my church as a teenager in the 1960s. As an urban pastor, I worked with families through recession and corporate layoffs of the 1970s and '80s, and conducted community interventions to prevent gang violence (Henry, Keys, Connelly, & Holstein, 1989).

Because of these life experiences, my interests in graduate school soon centered around family and community models. Fern Chertok introduced me to community psychology. My master's project concerned organizational and family systems factors related to stress among ministers (Henry, Chertok, Keys, & Jegerski, 1991). My Ph.D. studies at the University of Illinois were in the areas of organizational and social psychology, with a heavy methodology emphasis. There I worked with Christopher Keys and Jim Kelly, and still collaborate with both.

After finishing the course work for my Ph.D., I was recruited to direct the assessments for the "Metropolitan Area Child Study" (MACS), then in its first year of operation. The MACS was a research demonstration project testing three levels of increasingly intense interventions to prevent the emergence of aggression and antisocial behavior in a sample of urban, primarily minority children from 16 public schools.

Soon after graduation, I was invited to become a co-investigator on the MACS project, and eventually we obtained funding for two other research projects. As a result, I was offered and accepted a tenure-track position in the Department of Psychiatry at the University of Illinois/Chicago.

Currently, I am an Assistant Professor of Psychology in the Department of Psychiatry, and one of three co-investigators in the Families and Communities Research Group at the Institute for Juvenile Research. We started this group in the belief that important questions require collaborative efforts of investigators, and research with large, high risk, urban samples. We specialize in research related to risk among children in urban communities and the role of school factors, poverty, and neighborhood violence in family interactions, peer relations, stress, coping, and antisocial behavior. I am in charge of the data-gathering and analysis activities for the group. We are currently involved in three major research projects, namely:

(1) The Chicago Youth Development Study: A longitudinal prediction study of approximately 300 adolescent boys followed from 6th grade into young adulthood, oversampled for high risk.
(2) The SAFE Children Project: A prevention study of risk markers for substance abuse, including school bonding, academic achievement, family involvement, and impulse control. This study is based on the theory that risk is multiply determined by community, school, and family factors as well as individual predispositions. Our interventions consist of academic tutoring in phonics, and a family group intervention aimed at helping parents navigate the transition into school.
(3) The Metropolitan Area Child Study (MACS): At this writing, we are in the followup phase of MACS, aiming at following intervention and control children through adolescence to determine the long-term effects of the interventions on academic achievement, school withdrawal, substance abuse, and criminal behavior.

Ecology is a generative idea for me. I have been influenced by the ideas of Murray Bowen, Roger Barker and Jim Kelly with respect to the ways in which individuals and human systems interact. Several of my research interests are related to applications of ecological psychology to our projects. These include peer influences on individual behavior (Henry, Tolan, & Van Acker, 1997), the development of children's self-concepts in urban contexts, friendship network characteristics and classroom norms (Henry, Guerra, Huesmann, & VanAcker, in press). I also maintain interests in the epidemiology of psychological disorders among urban children (Tolan, Henry, Guerra, VanAcker, Huesmann, & Eron, under review; Tolan & Henry, 1996; Henry, Sheidow, Tolan & Gorman-Smith, 1997), and in attitudes toward, and perceptions of persons with disabilities (Henry, Keys, Jopp, & Balcazar, 1996; Henry, Keys, Balcazar & Jopp, 1996).

My time is spent primarily in three activities: (1) supervision, (2) seeking funding, and (3) data analysis and writing. The staff of the

Families and Communities Research Group consists of the three co-investigators, three post-doctoral persons, six graduate research assistants, five B.A. level persons, and several undergraduate students. Students and recent Ph.D.s work with us because their interests coincide with the interests of our group. They do much of the actual assessment, intervention, data management, and analysis for our projects, and in the process learn the complexities involved in community research and analysis. My role is to supervise the work of 10 of these staff members, and to stimulate their thinking in ways that help them grow in their own abilities. As a result, I serve on many of their master's and doctoral committees.

In our department, as in many psychiatry departments, each faculty member must fund his or her own position, either through clinical work, research, administration, or teaching. Currently, we have sufficient grant funding for our positions and those of the staff members who work with us, but funding is an ongoing concern. Developing and contributing to grant proposals is a major part of my work. In 1997, I wrote one major grant proposal myself, collaborated in writing four others, and helped write a pre-proposal for a center. I expect that this level of grant writing will be fairly consistent every year. It takes approximately $1.5 million per year to pay for the work we want to do, and we are always searching for funds.

In addition to supervision and proposal writing, I work with my collaborators on analyses for their projects, and take time to write articles and chapters in keeping with my own interests. Working with several senior collaborators who desire to analyze and publish from our data, it is easy to be overwhelmed by the demands. This is especially true when deadlines for grant submissions, conferences, and special issues are near. Methodologists are often the third or fourth authors on such submissions, and it is easy for one's own research interests to get lost or delayed. I have made it a personal rule to take Tuesday of each week as a day for writing. I do not always keep this promise, but it does allow me to keep my own projects moving. In 1997 I wrote three articles, one chapter, and three conference presentations, in addition to methodological work on my colleagues' projects.

I would describe my position as intense, demanding, stimulating, and one of the few places in life where I can get paid for working on important questions. My collaborators and I have relationships of mutual respect and trust, which allow us to have animated discussion and debate. Working with students and earlier-career people is a great joy for me, and although I miss teaching courses, I have ample opportunity to teach.

If you are a mid-career person considering study in community psychology, I would advise you to mine your life experiences for the kinds of questions that can quicken your interest and motivate you when the demands of graduate study seem overwhelming. Most of all, do not be afraid. I am happy I stuck my toe in the water.

## REFERENCES

Henry, D. Chertok, F., Keys, C., & Jegerski, J. (1991) Organizational and family systems factors in stress among ministers. *American Journal of Community Psychology, 19, 931-952.*

Henry, D., Guerra, N.G., Huesmann, L. R., & Van Acker, R. (in press) Normative influences on aggression in urban elementary school classrooms. *American Journal of Community Psychology.*

Henry, D., Keys, C., Connelly, C., and Holstein, M. (1989) Learning from a church and community intervention in gang conflict. Symposium Presentation at the Midwest Psychological Association Convention, Chicago, Illinois, May 5, 1989.

Henry, D., Keys, C. B., Jopp, D. & Balcazar, F. (1996) The Community Living Attitudes Scale: Development and psychometric properties. *Mental Retardation, 34, 149-158.*

Henry, D., Keys, C. B., Balcazar, F., & Jopp, D. (1996) The attitudes of community agency staff toward community living for persons with mental retardation. *Mental Retardation, 34, 367-379.*

Henry, D., Sheidow, A., Tolan, P.H., & Gorman-Smith, D. (1997, April) Patterns of comorbidity among urban minority children: Replication and developmental exploration. Paper presented at the Biennial Meeting of the Society for Research in Child Development, Washington, DC, April 5, 1997.

Henry, D., Tolan, P.H., & Van Acker, R. (1997, April) Friendship network characteristics and aggressive behavior. Paper presented at the Biennial Meeting of the Society for Research in Child Development, Washington, DC, April 6, 1997.

Tolan, P. & Henry, D. (1996) Patterns of psychopathology among urban poor children: Comorbidity and Aggression Effects. *Journal of Consulting and Clinical Psychology.*

Tolan, P., Henry, D., Guerra, N. G., Van Acker, R., Huesmann, L. R. & Eron, L. Patterns of psychopathology among urban poor children I: Community, age, ethnicity and gender effects. Manuscript under review.

# Research, Teaching, and Service in Applied, Multidisciplinary Academic Programs and in Community Organizations

Douglas D. Perkins

University of Utah

**SUMMARY.** The present paper describes a possible career path to research, teaching, and service in interdisciplinary academic departments (e.g., criminal justice and family and social policy/human and community development). Such employment has become an increasingly viable and interesting career route, given the increase in multidisciplinary applied social science programs and the limited availability of academic jobs in psychology departments, especially for non-clinical and non-experimental psychologists. Professional consultations to local government (e.g., housing, planning, and police departments) and non-profit organizations (community voluntary associations and lobby/technical assistance organizations) are also common in this career path. *[Article copies available for a fee from The Haworth Document Delivery Service: 1-800-342-9678. E-mail address: getinfo@haworthpressinc.com <Website: http://www.haworthpressinc.com>]*

**KEYWORDS.** Community psychology, multidisciplinary

---

Address correspondence to: Douglas D. Perkins, Environment & Behavior Area, FCS Department/AEB, University of Utah, Salt Lake City, UT 84112 (email: Perkins@FCS.Utah.edu).

[Haworth co-indexing entry note]: "Research, Teaching, and Service in Applied, Multidisciplinary Academic Programs and in Community Organizations." Perkins, Douglas D. Co-published simultaneously in *Journal of Prevention & Intervention in the Community* (The Haworth Press, Inc.) Vol. 19, No. 2, 2000, pp. 121-128; and: *Employment in Community Psychology: The Diversity of Opportunity* (ed: Clifford R. O'Donnell, and Joseph R. Ferrari) The Haworth Press, Inc., 2000, pp. 121-128. Single or multiple copies of this article are available for a fee from The Haworth Document Delivery Service [1-800-342-9678, 9:00 a.m. - 5:00 p.m. (EST). E-mail address: getinfo@haworthpressinc.com].

To understand, or at least not be surprised at, the number of community psychologists working in nontraditional settings (i.e., outside psychology departments and clinics), one need only seek in vain for community psychology in the contents of most introductory psychology texts. These (no doubt unavoidable) defections from psychology may be interpreted as a proselytizing strength of community psychology. This article describes some of the personal experiences that have fostered my optimism about the employment picture in community research and action and about its current and potential impact. Ironically, that impact may be more on the broader profession of psychology (e.g., the American Psychological Association's recent emphases of urban community problems and prevention) and on multidisciplinary fields of research and intervention than on academic psychology departments which house most of the programs in community psychology.

I have worked as a faculty member in interdisciplinary programs in criminal justice and, for the past nine years, in environment and behavior and family and consumer studies. These experiences have affirmed the explicitly ecological, political, and applied philosophy of science of my training as a community psychologist. That training (at New York University) involved an ecological/systemic (and explicitly non-clinical) approach to community-based theory, research, and action in mental health and social change. Ecological theory and research means analyzing the community social, political, economic, and physical environment of psychosocial problems. Systemic action implies the solution or prevention of those problems at the programmatic or policy, as opposed to individual treatment, level. What field could be more naturally interdisciplinary?

## *RESEARCH*

Most of my research interests lie in three areas: (1) processes of community social and environmental change via citizen participation in block and neighborhood organizations, (2) the impact of crime and social and environmental disorder on individuals and communities, and (3) the role of social research in societal change. Related topics include methods of analyzing the social and physical environment of neighborhoods, research dissemination and application, strategies of individual, organizational, and community empowerment, and neighborhood issues, such as housing (affordability, deterioration, revitalization, preservation), land use, environmental hazards, crime, delin-quency, and substance abuse. Settings include homes, residential street-blocks, community voluntary associations, neighborhoods, hu-man service agencies, and policy-making jurisdictions. These com-plex, "real-world" issues and settings require an ecological research orientation, careful attention to multiple levels of analysis, and, ideal-ly, multiple methods of data collection: in my case, telephone surveys and qualitative, in-depth interviews, physical environmental assess-ment, use of both quantitative and qualitative archives (crime records, census data, content analysis of newspaper articles), and program evaluation techniques. Indeed, to really understand these topics and methods, one must become interdisciplinary, at least in terms of read-ing the literature in many fields (community, social, developmental, and environmental psychology, sociology and demography, political science, economics, geography, urban affairs and planning, law, crimi-nology, community organizing and development). Keeping up with other disciplines is, of course, easier in a multidisciplinary department.

## TEACHING

I have taught the following courses at the University of Utah (descrip-tions on Worldwide Web at www.fcs.utah.edu/fcs/perkinsd.html): Social Research Methods, Community Environments, Community Psycholo-gy, Community and Environmental Change, Graduate Thesis Devel-opment Seminar, Capstone in Service-Learning (to allow students to conduct their own evaluation, need assessment, or other follow-up project in a setting where they have volunteered), Social Scientists and Social Policy, Community Service and the Needs of Children. Before coming to Utah, as a visiting professor at Temple University's Depart-ment of Criminal Justice, I taught: Community Crime Prevention, Environmental Criminology, Planned Organizational and Community Change, Urban Crime Patterns, Research Methods in Criminal Justice, and Introduction to Criminal Justice. Almost *all* of the above courses in both programs are very multidisciplinary. In fact, the only course I have ever taught (at Utah and as a graduate student at New York University) that is at all *intra*disciplinary is Community Psychology.

## SERVICE AND "SERVICE LEARNING"

Service learning (SL), a significant and growing movement in sec-ondary and higher education, is "a method under which students . . .

learn and develop through active participation in thoughtfully organized service that: is conducted in and meets the needs of a community
and is coordinated with . . . the community; helps foster civic responsibility; is integrated into and enhances the academic curriculum of the
students . . . ; and includes structured time for the students and participants to reflect on the service experience" (National and Community
Service Trust Act of 1993). SL students learn practical skills and
information, greater political awareness, and a more developed sense
of communitarianism. It adds reality and relevance to the curriculum
by bringing to life dry classroom materials, by showing how social
processes really work (and often do not work as planned) in the unpredictable and complex world of realpolitik, and by giving students skills, experience, and connections that often lead to employment opportunities.
(There is an SL listserv for students, faculty, SL coordinators, and job-
seekers (see website: <///csf.colorado.EDU:80/sl/main.html>). The National
Service-Learning Cooperative Clearinghouse (ERIC) website is at
<www.nicl.coled.umn.edu>. The campus Outreach Opportunity League
website is at <www.COOL2SERVE.org>. The International Partnership
for Service-Learning is at <www.studyabroad.com/psl>.)

I have incorporated service learning into almost all the courses I
have taught at Utah. About a thousand undergraduates and ten graduate students have helped plan, conduct, and report on my various
community service/research projects, which have provided useful information to a wide variety of public and private organizations (community councils, Neighborhood Housing Services, Community Services Council, an ecumenical religious service and advocacy
anti-poverty organization, and the SLC Council, Office of Housing
and Development, RDA, Planning and Police Departments, and Multi-
Ethnic Advisory Committee) with whom the students worked. The
projects also had a clearly positive and lasting impact on the students'
learning, as evidenced by their application of ideas and observations
from the project to later course work and by their anonymous comments on course evaluations.

## A PATH TO INTERDISCIPLINARY RESEARCH, TEACHING, AND SERVICE

The most effective strategy for both distinguishing oneself as a
student and getting a "foot in the door" for a job is to volunteer to

assist on faculty or off-campus research projects. For example, while a student at Swarthmore College in 1978, I contacted the Research and Evaluation Department at Hahnemann (now JFK) Mental Health Center in Philadelphia and offered to do a study of the impact of father absence on an inner-city adolescent clinical population. This led to my undergraduate thesis, supervised by Kenneth Gergen, on prevention as social policy. After college, while working as a residential psychiatric counselor I did my own independent research on learned helplessness and attributional style among delinquent and mentally ill adolescents.

After discovering the limitations inherent in individual-level, medical-model interventions to solve problems that are as environmental, institutional, legal, and political as they are psychological, my career interests shifted accordingly. I enrolled in the doctoral program in community psychology at New York University instead of a clinical or even clinical-community program. This shift in orientation is also evidenced in my master's thesis project (under Marybeth Shinn) evaluating an elementary school interpersonal problem-solving primary prevention program, taking elective courses in sociology and the law, and my article on the role for community psychologists in public interest litigation (Perkins, 1988).

## RESEARCH ON PRACTICAL COMMUNITY PROBLEMS AND RESPONSES

In 1984, I met David Chavis at the first Northeast Community Psychology conference at NYU and mentioned that my tentative dissertation topic was on community crime prevention. He explained that he, Paul Florin, Richard Rich, and Abraham Wandersman were planning a Ford Foundation project on the role of block associations in community development and crime control. I volunteered to spearhead the collection of environmental and crime data for that project in exchange for access to all project data for my dissertation. (I even wrote a contract signed by the Principal Investigators and myself and delineating responsibilities and authorship arrangements, which I would encourage all student-faculty research teams to do.) This soon led to a paid position for me as a research associate with the Citizens Committee for New York City, which administered the Ford grant (see Perkins & Wandersman, 1990).

Around that time, I independently wrote two small grant proposals (to the National Institute of Justice and Society for the Psychological Study of Social Issues) to fund my dissertation on "The Social and Physical Environment of Residential Blocks, Crime and Citizens' Participation in Block Associations" (Shinn and Barbara Felton, advisors). Both grants were funded and my thesis won the 1991 Dissertation Award of APA Division 27: the Society for Community Research and Action. That work led to several articles (Perkins et al., 1990; Perkins et al., 1993; Perkins, Brown & Taylor, 1996) and many conference papers.

In developing the Block Environmental Inventory, a new instrument to measure the crime-related physical environment of streetblocks, for my dissertation, I sought the advice of Ralph Taylor in the Criminal Justice Department at Temple University. This turned out to be an inadvertently good career move. The following year, Taylor hired me to direct a National Institute of Mental Health study of stress and coping with urban crime and fear. That job gave me valuable skills and experience in planning and managing a large, multi-method research project, including training and supervising research assistants. I co-authored the voluminous Final Report to NIMH and several articles and conference papers on fear of crime, the physical environment of urban neighborhoods, and citizen participation in community organizations (Perkins, Meeks & Taylor, 1992; Taylor et al., 1995; Perkins & Taylor, 1996; Perkins et al., 1996). That experience made me much more marketable as both an academic and an applied researcher.

That project lasted three years, but only funded a Director for one year. So a year into the project, I started my first full-time teaching job as a Visiting Assistant Professor of Criminal Justice for two years. Although this allowed me to hone my teaching skills, learn some interesting, but unfamiliar subjects, and continue work on both the NIMH project and my doctoral dissertation, it also gave me much more empathy for those forced to work two or more (in my case, essentially three full-time) jobs. Like other adults, most graduate students have bills to pay. So I fell into the common pitfall of not finishing my dissertation *before* moving on to a new job and research project, which is my only caution and regret about that experience. It took an intensive effort to simultaneously finish the dissertation and NIMH project and teach four courses per semester. But doing so helped me find the perfect person-environment fit: a tenure-track job as a community and environmental psychologist in a multidisciplinary, applied research-oriented program in a good institution and high quality-of-life setting.

## POLICY RESEARCH

Policy research has long provided employment opportunities for community psychologists. My policy-related research and consulting has been in the areas of community development and housing and crime, delinquency, and drug abuse prevention at the local level. After studying community crime prevention strategies in New York City and Philadelphia, I have consulted with police departments on community-oriented policing practices. I also helped write grant proposals to the National Institute of Justice and the Office of Substance Abuse Prevention (OSAP) for the Eisenhower Foundation for the Prevention of Violence. In 1989, I authored an Eisenhower Foundation report reviewing its national Neighborhood Program Evaluation Conference, which critically analyzed community program evaluation research procedures. Since coming to Utah, I have conducted a variety of applied research projects, including (with Barbara Brown) a longitudinal study to evaluate a multi-million-dollar HUD/Salt Lake City community revitalization project in two working-class neighborhoods (Perkins et al., 1996). I have also consulted on two national OSAP evaluation proposals and the evaluation of the Salt Lake Valley Drug Abuse Prevention Coalition Community Partnership. All of these experiences, from my undergraduate days on, have allowed me to move freely between academia and the world of policy and practice.

## CONCLUSIONS

Academia tends to consider research, teaching, and service to be separate domains, but this is misleading for most community psychologists. What is perhaps unusual about academic community psychology is the degree to which *research, teaching, and community service work are inextricably intertwined.* For most academics, service consists of committee work in their department, university, and professional organization and it is an insignificant part of their duties and criteria for tenure and promotion. Community service is viewed at best as a public relations opportunity for the institution and at worst as a distraction from the primary purposes of academia: research first and teaching second.

But as a community psychologist, volunteering for program and policy planning or evaluation, or simply going to talk to community groups and policy-makers has been essential to my training, professional role, and social, political, and moral philosophy. This has led me to be involved in many class and independent projects that are primarily program evaluations, organization development surveys, or community need assessments. Most of these do not lead easily to journal publications. Although there are service and important teaching aspects of these projects, however, they are still valuable *research* studies for their direct utility to the organizations involved and for the theoretical and practical (e.g., data access) groundwork laid for future research. Although community service and service learning can be time consuming, they not only benefit my department and institution in their relations with the community, they are also of tremendous help to my research and teaching and to many of my students who, like me, have launched their own careers through such projects. Interdisciplinary programs seem to appreciate and reward this more than psychology departments, it's sad but not surprising to say, even those with community programs.

## REFERENCES

Perkins, D.D. (1988). The use of social science in public interest litigation: A role for community psychologists. *American Journal of Community Psychology, 16,* 465-485.

Perkins, D.D., Brown, B.B., & Taylor, R.B. (1996). The ecology of empowerment: Predicting participation in community organizations. *Journal of Social Issues, 52,* 85-110.

Perkins, D.D., Florin, P., Rich, R.C., Wandersman, A. & Chavis, D.M. (1990). Participation and the social and physical environment of residential blocks: Crime and community context. *American Journal of Community Psychology, 17,* 83-115.

Perkins, D.D., Meeks, J.W., & Taylor, R.B. (1992). The physical environment of street blocks and resident perceptions of crime and disorder: Implications for theory and measurement. *Journal of Environmental Psychology, 12,* 21-34.

Perkins, D.D., & Taylor, R.B. (1996). Ecological assessments of community disorder: Their relationship to fear of crime and theoretical implications. *American Journal of Community Psychology, 24,* 63-107.

Perkins, D.D., & Wandersman, A. (1990). "You'll have to work to overcome our suspicions:" Benefits and pitfalls of research with community organizations. *Social Policy, 21 (1),* 32-41.

Perkins, D.D., Wandersman, A., Rich, R.C., & Taylor, R.B. (1993). The physical environment of street crime: Defensible space, territoriality and incivilities. *Journal of Environmental Psychology, 13,* 29-49.

Taylor, R.B., Koons, B.A., Kurtz, E.M., Greene, J.R., & Perkins, D.D. (1995). Street blocks with more nonresidential land use have more physical deterioration: Evidence from Baltimore and Philadelphia. *Urban Affairs Review, 31,* 120-136.

# Diversity of Opportunity, Consensus of Experience

Clifford R. O'Donnell

University of Hawaii

Joseph R. Ferrari

DePaul University

**KEYWORDS.** Community psychology, employment, multi-disciplinary

The authors of these articles have exemplified the diversity of opportunity in community psychology employment. Whether in applied, research, or academic settings, the variety of positions and the enthusiasm with which they are described is remarkable. Particularly noteworthy are the graduate students who are doing exciting work with Indigenous people, in independent consultation, and in collaborative action research, while they support themselves and complete graduate school. In addition to academic psychology positions and research centers, graduates of community psychology programs are employed in many less-traditional settings, including United Way, a University Affiliated Program for disability studies, public schools, government, non-profit organizations, medical schools, and interdisciplinary academic departments.

Address correspondence to: Clifford R. O'Donnell, Department of Psychology, University of Hawaii, Honolulu, HI 96822.

[Haworth co-indexing entry note]: "Diversity of Opportunity, Consensus of Experience." O'Donnell, Clifford R., and Joseph R. Ferrari. Co-published simultaneously in *Journal of Prevention & Intervention in the Community* (The Haworth Press, Inc.) Vol. 19, No. 2, 2000, pp. 129-131; and: *Employment in Community Psychology: The Diversity of Opportunity* (ed: Clifford R. O'Donnell, and Joseph R. Ferrari) The Haworth Press, Inc., 2000, pp. 129-131. Single or multiple copies of this article are available for a fee from The Haworth Document Delivery Service [1-800-342-9678, 9:00 a.m. - 5:00 p.m. (EST). E-mail address: getinfo@haworthpressinc.com].

With the diversity of employment, there is considerable consensus on the skills, concepts, and graduate school experiences that best prepared graduates for employment in community research and action. The types of preparation most emphasized were research/program evaluation and multi-disciplinary courses/experiences. Not surprisingly, research and evaluation skills were described as highly valued by employers and often considered essential to perform the activities of their positions. Statistics, grant-writing, and qualitative analysis, were the specific skills mentioned as most useful in conducting research and evaluation in the employment settings described in these articles.

More surprising was the strong appreciation of the importance of multi-disciplinary courses and experiences. Perhaps this is because most of the authors are not employed in traditional academic positions in psychology, but are working in multi-disciplinary content areas such as health, youth, families, disabilities, crime, social services, public policy, and social justice. In these positions they work with professionals from many disciplines and recognize the value of their ability to address issues from the perspective of another discipline, and the collaboration, participation, and consultation skills that they developed in community psychology. The experiences of these authors support the likelihood of the growth of interdisciplinary graduate programs noted in our review of education in community psychology (O'Donnell & Ferrari, 1997).

There is also consensus on the value of the traditional concepts of community psychology. The importance of empowerment, prevention, advocacy, values, social networks/support, systems change, community strengths, self-help, and community development in community education and employment was expressed throughout these articles.

The experiences of these authors provide useful information to graduate students and graduate program faculty. Their advice is for graduate students to:

1. take courses outside of psychology
2. develop knowledge and skills in a content area
3. acquire research and program evaluation experience
4. develop skills in statistics, qualitative analysis, grant-writing, interviewing, consultation, and publishing
5. volunteer for the research and practicum experience needed
6. seek a practicum placement with a prospective employer

7. consider the value of possible dissertation topics to prospective employers
8. consider non-traditional employment settings
9. realistically assess the value of their knowledge and skills to prospective employers
10. view their career as an evolutionary process

There was also advice for seeking employment. Many authors noted the importance of relationships in obtaining their positions. Often these relationships were developed in research and community placements, and through professional activities. The most specific advice, offered by Campbell, Angelique, BootsMiller, and Davidson, was to form a job club with a faculty advisor and other graduate students seeking employment. They applied the principles of community psychology of collaboration, network development, social support, and empowerment to the process and were highly successful. The idea and curriculum that they developed would be useful in every community graduate program.

This special issue and book began with the questions "What can you do with a graduate degree in community psychology?" and "Who employs community psychologists?" These authors have provided outstanding examples of answers to these questions. The insightful conclusions of Campbell, Angelique, BootsMiller, and Davidson are informative: "in the process of applying for jobs and interviewing, we learned that our training and skills had provided a foundation for success in many employment settings. With a little network development, unlimited positions for community psychologists seemed to exist. . . We came to understand that there are a variety of settings in which community psychologists are employable, and that we each fit best in different settings. Rather than viewing the field as small and limited, we came to see community psychology as growing and expansive."

## REFERENCE

O'Donnell, C. R., & Ferrari, J. R. (1997). Undergraduate courses and graduate programs in community research and action: Issues and future directions. In C. R. O'Donnell & J. R. Ferrari, (Eds.), *Education in community psychology: Models for graduate and undergraduate programs* (pp. 97-99). New York: The Haworth Press, Inc.

# Index